STAR CHAMBER STORIES

Star Chamber Stories

G. R. ELTON

LONDON

METHUEN & CO LTD

BARNES & NOBLE BOOKS

NEW YORK

First published in 1958
This edition reprinted 1974 by
Methuen & Co Ltd
11 New Fetter Lane
London EC4P 4EE
and Barnes & Noble Books, New York
10 East 53rd Street
New York NY 10022
(a division of Harper & Row Inc.)
Printed in Great Britain by
Whitstable Litho, Straker Brothers Ltd

Methuen SBN 416 80940 5

Barnes & Noble SBN 06 471943 X

CONTENTS

★

ACKNOWLEDGMENTS

Earlier versions of numbers III and V have appeared in the *Cambridge Historical Journal* for 1954 and the *Journal of Ecclesiastical History* for 1956, respectively; I wish to thank the editors and publishers of those journals for their kind permission to include them here. I should also like to thank those who have generously allowed me to use material for the pictures; their names are given on the opposite page.

ILLUSTRATIONS

between pages 112 and 113

John Parkins to the Abbot of Osney
> (*Star Chamber Proceedings, 2/34/11, by courtesy of the Public Record Office, London*)

A Plan of Cambridge, *c.* 1550
> (*From John Caius*, De Antiquitate Cantabrigiensis Academiae, *1574; by kind permission of the Librarian, Gonville and Caius College, Cambridge*)

Sir Brian Tuke, *c.* 1540
> (*by Hans Holbein the yr.; from the Mellon Collection, Washington National Gallery*)

The Parish Church of St. Mary's, Hayes, Middx.
> (*from a photograph in the possession of the Rev. A. E. Hill, M.A., sometime Rector of Hayes, and by his kind permission*)

INTRODUCTION

The six essays collected in this volume have only two things in common: they all concern themselves with the middle years of Henry VIII's reign, and they have some connection – close or distant – with the court of Star Chamber. These common features they owe to their origin, for they are, in effect, by-products of a larger enterprise. While investigating the history of the early-Tudor Council in all its aspects and with all its accompanying institutions (a labour of many years on which I am now embarked) I ran across indications here and there that the papers of Star Chamber might contain materials for the telling of stories of a kind which historians of the sixteenth century are only rarely lucky enough to find. For once, the familiar but faintly unreal paths of historical study looked like running through reasonably open country where normally they are hemmed in by a forest impenetrable in its gloomy and permanent obscurity. It proved possible, for a little while, to get away both from the towering figures of political history and from the abstractions of the economic and social historian – possible to learn something about people who would never ordinarily make the headlines but who, living in the sixteenth century, got involved with the law and thus preserved themselves for posterity.

The particular stories which are presented here are not the only ones that could be told. The records of Star

Chamber and Chancery will reward the willing searcher with many similar, and possibly even fuller, tales of the more or less obscure. I have picked these six in part because they fall within the period of history with which at present my interests are chiefly bound up, and in part because they seem to me to combine sufficient of the two ideal qualities for which I was looking: they were to be good stories in their own right, but they should also have some light to throw on the history of their day. I may well be cherishing illusions, but it seems to me that at least five of them offer means of testing some of the generalizations which we necessarily apply to historical writing, and of correcting misconceptions only too likely to occur where history becomes divorced from knowledge of detail. That they throw light on the lives, the habits and the speech of men and women in the sixteenth century goes without saying, though it may be as well to remember that evidence of life which is taken from legal records is always a little distorted. But it was a litigious century, and few there were who never rubbed shoulders with the officers of the law. I should, perhaps, mention that all the words quoted in the book are taken straight from the record. If an element of fiction or improbability seems sometimes to creep in, the fault is not mine; either the lawyers of the time were given to writing fiction, or our preconceptions are wrong. On the other hand, though I usually prefer a more austere practice, I have decided not to burden the reader with too many sixteenth-century vagaries and have throughout modernized the spelling and punctuation. I have done so the more readily because the majority of my quotations, taken from legal records, enshrine only the speech of the man in question; the writing is that of some clerk or lawyer.

One of these stories has little enough 'national' significance, but it is here partly because of the duty I owe to the University which has been so generous to me, and partly because it has done most to reassure me that others, too, may find these tales amusing and interesting. 'Cambridge Riots' has been heard by many, and all have been kind to it. I owe them all great thanks, particularly to one friend who is willing (so he says) to hear it a fourth time. I cannot either understand or approve this quirk, but it has played its part in encouraging me to present these tales to the public. Others of the stories have also been read to audiences whose kindness demands a general expression of gratitude. No one, however, need feel at all responsible for the fact that the stories are now appearing in print: that responsibility, and any blame attaching to it, is entirely mine.

As I have said, all the stories have some connection with the records of Star Chamber, but there are marked differences. As far as Nos. I, IV, and V are concerned, Star Chamber comes into it only inasmuch as among its records may be found surprising odds and ends which have put me on the track of the story behind them. The remaining three essays, on the other hand, involved proper suits in the court. The reason for these differences lies in the nature of Star Chamber at this time, and a word on this subject may prove helpful for an understanding of the technicalities which might otherwise make the stories themselves difficult to follow. It is of course true that the history of Star Chamber under the early Tudors remains uncertain and obscure, despite some work done on it; that is why I am engaged in a task which includes that court. Nevertheless, some things can even now be said about it with fair confidence. In the first place, it must once again be stressed that Star Chamber does not deserve its evil reputation. Though this is now a commonplace among historians, popular opinion may not yet have caught up with this revision of an ancient legend. Under the Tudors, at least, the court commanded great popularity because it offered remedies for grievances and complaints not catered for by the regular (common law) courts, because it was impartial between contenders, because it could not be intimidated by the strong or bribed by the rich, and because it brought to its decisions the weight of high authority. With regard to this last, however, it seems likely that historians have seriously overestimated its efficiency. It is certainly surprising to find that of the few extant decrees issued by the court quite a number order a man to observe an earlier Star Chamber decree. The court was a necessary and formidable weapon in establishing respect for the law in the land, but the task itself was even more formidable. Genuine obedience to and deference for the law were not English characteristics until the nineteenth century, when it became really difficult to avoid being found out.

In essence, the court of Star Chamber consisted of the king's Council sitting as a court; in practice its members were the leading councillors and especially the lord chancellor, its president. It sat in term time only (the legal terms extended through sixteen weeks in the year), in a room in the palace of Westminster called the Star Chamber. Its jurisdiction covered mainly riots, but other offences against law-enforcement – false jury verdicts, perjury, contempt of court – were also subject to it; and since any dispute could be turned into an alleged riot by including in the charge the raising of bands or the carrying of weapons, the court's sphere of action spread rapidly and wide. But though matters before it always involved some measure of violence, real or pretended, it was not in the technical sense a criminal court: it could not deal with felonies and treasons, and therefore could not award the penalty of death. Its usual weapons were fines and (in extreme cases) imprisonment at pleasure, but most commonly it simply pontificated, relying on the weight of the authority embodied in the Council, that is the government. Star Chamber did not use torture nor, under the early Tudors, corporal punishments or such weapons of ridicule as the pillory.

In this description I have spoken as though by the middle of Henry VIII's reign the court had achieved indisputable existence, and that is indeed what I believe to be the truth. However, there is much debate and uncertainty about this. The fundamental problem lies in the difficulty of distinguishing between the Council as a deliberative, executive and investigatory body, and the councillors in Star Chamber comprising a recognized and regular court of the realm. Some historians would deny that the distinction ever became complete before the abolition of the court in 1641; others cannot see it before 1570. There has also been much discussion on the origins of the court, though that is a question which does not concern us here. I am not denying that two institutions staffed by essentially the same people may be hard to keep apart; both the members themselves and later observers must at times have found it difficult to say with which aspect of the body they were dealing. For one statement found in many textbooks is definitely wrong: there was never any division within the king's Council between those who governed as members of the Privy Council and those who adjudicated upon law-suits in Star Chamber. There was a distinction, before the organization of the restricted Privy Council in 1536–40, between greater and lesser councillors, but only the greater mattered both in Council and in Star Chamber. The real difference between the two institutions lay mainly in their organization: after 1540 each had its own clerk keeping its own series of archives.

After that date, therefore, the institutional existence of the court of Star Chamber is certain; it cannot be assumed with equal assurance before that. But it must be said that anyone working through the records of the 1520s and 1530s will soon gather a conviction that contemporaries believed in the existence of something to be called the court of Star Chamber. Since this was to them not a problem of constitutional niceties but a question of where they would have their legal disputes settled, we may for once accept contemporary opinion as sound. If they thought that the Council in Star Chamber was really a court, then – to all intents – it was such a court. The immemorial jurisdiction of the Council, available to resolve difficulties (on the king's behalf) and answer the subject's petitions, over and beyond the competence of the regular courts, had been channelled by the work of Henry VII and especially of Wolsey into the flexible but predictable jurisdiction of a special court. Although much yet remains to be done and proved in this matter where all the standard accounts are rendered unreliable by their dependence on a small selection from the great mass of evidence, it may tentatively be said here that for practical purposes there was a regular court of Star Chamber, sitting at Westminster and composed of the leading councillors, by the time that Wolsey fell from power (1529).

However, it is also true that the close link between Council and Star Chamber left its mark, and the records of the early Tudor Star Chamber are complicated by that fact. Among them may be found papers which had little or nothing to do with the Council as a regular court; they are there because they reached the Council in its capacity

as the government of the realm. It is for that reason that
the study of Star Chamber archives has led me to some
stories which do not touch the formal and public judicial
work of the court. The material belongs to the Council,
a body sufficiently flexible and sufficiently wide in its con
cerns to bring almost any secular matter in the realm
under its review; and – as Nos. V and VI show – matters
spiritual were also far from excluded. But this confusion
in the records, this interaction of the Council in its various
capacities, does not alter the fact that the regular court of
Star Chamber was one of these capacities.

One last word must be said about the archives from
which so much of the material for these stories is drawn.
Procedure in Star Chamber was affected by that of Chancery, not surprisingly since the lord chancellor presided
in both. It was in English, where the common law used
a form of French, and in writing; moreover, it was rela-
tively informal so that a man would not lose his rights
because he had offended some technicality or because no
formula existed to cover his case, both of which troubles
were often encountered at common law. A Star Chamber
suit began with the putting in of plaintiff's bill, a document in which he stated the nature of the dispute or
grievance, described its history, and appealed to the lords
of the Council for redress. This was followed by defendant's answer which asserted that the case ought to be tried
at common law, that nevertheless defendant was willing to
abide by the decision of Star Chamber, that there was no
truth in the bill, and that the suit should be dismissed with
costs to defendant. To this plaintiff entered his replication
while defendant was given his chance to come back with
a rejoinder; sometimes a third pair of documents appeared
with the rebuttal and surrebuttal. But it is very rare indeed
for any document after the bill and answer to produce new

points; by the early seventeenth century it was recognized that they could not do so, and the later stages, now purely formal, were continued only because officers of the court earned fees through them. The essence of a Star Chamber trial lay in the examination of witnesses, at that time a method almost unknown to the common law. After the putting in of formal complaints and replies, both parties were usually ordered to supply interrogatories (or sets of questions) to which answers should be obtained from a list of witnesses named by them. On the basis of these depositions, which often included some from the party accused, and any other evidence available to it, the court made up its mind and announced its decision or decree.

This summarized statement has simplified a great deal. There is the problem of summoning accused, done by the writ of *subpoena*, first under the privy seal and later under the great seal; usually, after the collection of the written evidence, there was a public trial in which counsel for the parties went verbally over the ground already covered in writing; in a majority of cases the court delegated some or all the stages – the taking of an answer, the taking of depositions, sometimes even the settlement of a dispute – to local commissioners by empowering writs of *dedimus potestatem*. But these and other details, important and interesting as they are, cannot here be discussed at length. What matters are the archives produced by the written proceedings: bill, answer, replication, rejoinder, interrogatory, depositions, decree.

Apart from the collections of these papers, the court kept a proper and formal record in the so-called books of orders and decrees in which its resolutions were entered at all stages, from the decision to submit the defendant to his answer to the final decree. Unfortunately, however, these books disappeared in the civil wars of the seventeenth century and have not been seen since. What survives are the actual papers or proceedings, but few of these are complete. They had no evidential value later on – could not be cited in any court as evidence – and were kept without much care as files bundled up in packages; in the nineteenth century some were sorted out and bound in volumes, but this has only added to the confusion. Ideally, one should find all the stages of the process, including writs ordering the taking of depositions and the like, and with luck even a draft decree might have slipped in with the file. In practice, a good many of the relevant documents are commonly missing. Since the books of orders and decrees are totally lost, it is sadly true that we almost never know what the court decided in the end. The reconstruction of a Star Chamber case is therefore attended by every sort of difficulty. The stories that follow were made possible only by the fact that in these particular cases rather more of the proceedings survive than is usual, and also by the existence of auxiliary evidence in other parts of the public records. Time and again we shall have to admit that we can only conjecture the truth of the statements recorded or guess at the court's decision. This does not render the reconstruction invalid: it makes it more difficult but also more exciting to do. And we might also remember that though we should know more about the work and standing of the court if we had the decrees but none of the proceedings, we should also know very much less about the lives, the attitudes and the speech of a vanished age, of which rare and valuable knowledge the records of Star Chamber vouchsafe so many surprising and significant details.

THE FOOL OF OXFORD

A deplorable story

Few notions about the age of Henry VIII's break with Rome are more familiar and more solidly entrenched than that it witnessed a reign of terror. Casual words of no real significance (so runs the story) brought harmless men and women to the attention of the authorities, and once a man had been delated to Thomas Cromwell or his minions his fate was sealed. To quote the author who has perhaps done more than anyone to create this general impression: 'The punishments in these cases were very severe: there are almost no records of the penalties inflicted on those against whom the depositions were brought, but there is reason to believe that comparatively slight misdemeanours were not seldom rewarded with death.' [1] Mr Merriman offered no support for this categorical deduction from missing evidence, but this has not prevented common acceptance of his views. The truth is that he was venting his feelings, not arguing a case. As a rule it is indeed hard to discover what became of the many about whom informations were laid before magistrates or the Council, though common sense suggests that a conviction with penalty (especially an execution) is less likely to go unrecorded than the fact that nothing was done about some poor man who had talked silly in his cups. One may make allowance for the feelings of honourable men in settled times, striving in vain to understand a revolution, but it is not so easy to forgive scholarship as slipshod as this. However, what matters, of course, is not that errors should be shown up but that more should be known, and here the story of John Parkins' quarrel in January 1537 with the abbots of Eynsham and Osney will assist.

The protagonists are men of some interest. Parkins (or Perkins)* was a lawyer who died round about 1545. The date of his birth is not known, but in 1537 he referred to events twenty years back as though he had then already been engaged in his profession. He is thus unlikely to have been born much later than 1490, and the fact that he did not supplicate for the degrees of B.Can.L. and B.C.L. until 1528–9[2] must be explained by his originally leaving Oxford without a degree, as Anthony à Wood tells us he did.[3] Wood says that he was 'born of genteel parents, and being naturally inclin'd to good letters, was sent to the university, and there carefully trained up in grammar and logic'. On going down he became a member of the Inner Temple where 'he made a wonderful proficiency in the common law, was called to the bar, practised the law, and was much resorted to for his counsel'. His fame rests in the main on a textbook – *A profitable booke treating of the lawes of England* – in which he analysed the law of conveyancing. First published in French in 1528 (and in an English translation in 1555), this little book ran through fifteen editions in the sixteenth century[4] and was republished as late as 1827. However, successful as

* Perkins is the version of *D.N.B.*, Foster, &c., but as he invariably used the 'a' himself and therefore pronounced his name like modern Parkins, not Perkins, I have adopted this spelling.

Parkins may at first have been in his legal career, there are indications that he had come a cropper before we meet him in 1537. By then he was clearly resident and practising at Oxford, which was quite a decline from his London days; also, as we shall see, he was showing signs of a crotchety quarrelsome disposition and a mind disturbed into incoherence and even near-madness. Perhaps these traits were connected with his downfall: he himself relates a story current about him that round about 1517 'my heels was turned upward and my head downward in Westminster Hall, and so banished the Hall'.[5] He denied the story – 'O admirabile scandalum' – but if it was true (and if such ceremonies were really employed in drumming a man out of the centre of England's legal system) it would certainly help to explain his later state of mind.

Parkins' views, and especially the line he took over the critical issues of those years, appear from three pieces of his writing – the preface to his book and two papers he sent to Cromwell. The preface[6] reveals him as a man trained in jurisprudence and eager to speculate about first principles. Being concerned with property law, he first defined possession and property as a consequence of the Fall, after which communism was rendered dangerous to peace (*pacifica conversatio*) and to necessary sustentation: the greed of strong men would threaten the former and deprive weaker men of the latter, unless the law defined each man's possessions precisely. He cited Aristotle against Plato, played about with the laws natural and divine, and gave a clear account of the law human or positive. To be just, this last law requires in the legislator both wisdom and authority, wisdom to ensure conformity with right reason and authority because 'dicitur lex a ligendo'. He went on to analyse authority into paternal and political, the former being based on the law of nature and the latter vested in one person or the community by something very like an original contract. Men create authority by election and agreement, for they can and must so submit themselves in all things not contrary to God's law. The Bible is quoted – Noah's division of land among his sons after the Flood, and Abraham's agreement with Lot – to prove that things very probably happened in this way. Not content with touching in his three or four pages on all the major bases of the conventional jurisprudence of his day, he went on to show himself aware of the relativity of human laws: 'in legibus aliquid dandum est consuetudini temporis et patriae et moribus hominum.' This little preface certainly testifies both to the 'admirable education' which Wood complacently says Parkins had received at Oxford, and to the reasons for his success as a lawyer.

The book was written before 1528; one cannot help feeling that the two schemes he composed in 1537 show his mental powers much reduced, though his ingenuity remained great. The first of them was a 'politic means how to destroy the rebellious traitors in the north parts', that is, the pilgrims of grace.[7] The essence of this was that some faithful men must pretend to be traitors and 'sub colore amicicie et cum fidei vultu' penetrate the pilgrims' ranks. He offered examples of the sort of talk with which they could win the rebels' confidence, as that the king's commander was ready to come over with many men and part of his ordnance. These agents' efforts must be supported by having them proclaimed traitors in towns near the rebel host. After they have established themselves they shall make the rebels split up into small and widely dispersed groups over which they can easily gain control. 'Diverse other means may be imagined.' They can get the rebels to fire their beacons and thus make them gather together at certain points; in the meantime some king's troops can burn the deserted houses and kill all the women and children. Another way would be to recruit traitors among the rebels themselves. The letter is signed 'with the shaking hand of your honourable lordship's daily orator John Parkyns, impotent of body to labour but (thanks be to God and to your honourable lordship) yet alive and whole of mind and perfect memory'. Perhaps so: one wonders. Anyway, in its imaginitive detail, bloodthirstiness, stressing of the obvious and general impracticability (not to say idiocy), the scheme displays to perfection the mind of the inexperienced man of letters planning war. Parkins might have written some good thrillers; in fact, when his tussle with the abbots has been related, it may well be thought that he did. But what cannot be in doubt is his unswerving devotion to the cause of the king and to the new state of affairs in the Church, also witnessed by the fact that in all his voluminous letters and depositions every mention of the king is invariably and tediously followed by the words 'God save his grace'.

The other scheme is both longer and more important. It presents suggestions for reorganizing the universities and for secularizing further ecclesiastical property.[8] Hatred of priests and preference for laymen ran right through it. In the first place, Parkins thought that the head of every college should be a 'faithful subject of the king's grace . . . being no priest but a politic wise man'. He was to have exclusive control of all college property and the college seal, to enjoy the fines and profits collected by manorial courts on college estates, and to appoint all college officers 'and counsellors' – a hint that Parkins may possibly have fallen out with a college which looked elsewhere for its legal advice. After a survey had been made of the college's revenues (based on the last seven years' income), the master was to have an allowance for the whole college and he alone was to deal with 'the payment of the brewers, bakers and all manner of victuallers'. He was to hold office by royal appointment – by letters patent made out 'quamdiu nobis placeunt' (that is, during plea-sure); fellows and scholars were to be appointed in the same way, while the master would make 'conducts and Querestars', that is, priests appointed to conduct the ser-vices and choristers. Out of the surplus revenue not put aside for the running of the college, the master was to equip a number of 'good archers and other fighting-men', the number being fixed by the king's Council; he was to have no other servants, 'the only child of his chamber except'. Here Parkins' love for detail got the better of him. He ordered the master to provide for every archer 'a good bow and a good sheaf of arrows, an Armeynge [German] sword and an Armeygne dagger, and a half-penny purse with twenty shillings of groats, half-groats, and pence in it, to spend in the king his grace's affairs'. Other servants would get 'a good halberd or a good pole-axe, a good Armeynge sword and a good Armeynge dagger', and the same purse with contents. Moreover, all these troops were to have 'a soldier's coat ready hanging by his harness [equipment] and a good horse or gelding in the stable'. The purpose of these martial preparations is not explained; perhaps Parkins was thinking of the rebellion in Yorkshire or aware of the difficulties experi-enced by Tudor governments in raising armies, difficulties they sometimes tried to solve by statutes designed to main-tain trained forces in private households. His next point was more obvious: after all expenses paid and sufficient plate saved for the master, the king was to have all the remaining plate and revenue of the college.

This major proposal, by which the universities* would have lost their independence and come under the control of royal officials, was followed by a mixed bag of other reforms. On all feast-days the masters of colleges shall provide preachers in the neighbouring parishes to 'preach sincerely the gospel or epistle of that day'. Their efforts were to be supplemented in the university itself by six special preachers, doctors and bachelors of divinity, chosen (an interesting point) from the friars and receiving a royal dispensation enabling them to devote themselves to this single task. 'And every such doctor and bachelor of divinity will be glad to take four marks' stipend, their livery-gown cloth, their chambers and barbers and commons etc.' – as well they might. This concern for the preaching of the gospel is significant of Parkins' inclination to the newer ways of thinking; a little further on, however, he expresses himself in favour of continuing 'all exequies, masses and other devout prayers' as they had been used. He was no extremist or even Lutheran, though clearly hostile to the old priesthood. The canons of Christ Church ('the king his grace's college') were also to make way for 'politic wise' laymen and to live together in the 'new builded house – they have a fair kitchen for their cooks'. A violent attack is made on the canon and civil lawyers of New College (who are to be reduced in numbers), of Peckwater's Inn, owned by New College, whose company of law students was to be dispersed and the place used as an almshouse, and of other lawyers' halls, as Broadgates, Hinksey Hall, Edward Hall, and Wright Hall. Of course, Parkins was a common lawyer of whom such an outburst is to be expected; but he had also once studied the canon and civil laws and as late as 1528–9 had tried

* Though Parkins ostensibly concerned himself with both universities, it is quite plain that he was exclusively interested in Oxford.

to get degrees in those subjects. Had his supplication failed? There is no record of his proceeding to a degree, and this disappointment may well be behind his present violence.

Next, Parkins made some points which strongly suggest that all was not well with his sanity. All these proposals for the secularizing of the universities and depriving them of their revenues were, no doubt, extravagant, but they had some grounding in sense and public policy. What, however, shall we make of his eager attack on academic dress, especially hoods or even boots 'when they proceed [go in procession] ne at other times'? He wished all members of the university to wear 'secular raiment named layman's raiment'. The reason he gave was waste of cloth. Worse still, there is his almost incomprehensible assault on the bedells' staffs. Their bedells, he cries, go before their doctors

> with a clubbed staff and a peak [pike?] in the end, intending to hold by conquest; for the clubbed end with the peak in it is upward, and the staff upon the bedell's shoulder ready to strike. And once a year the company of the halls in Oxford goeth to the wood and cometh home through the town of Oxford with every man a club on his shoulder etc. And what arms the bedells' staff hath upon the smaller end I cannot certify to your honourable lordship, but one Daniel Pratt, a very honest man, one of the bailiffs of the town of Oxford and now being within the precinct of the City of London, as I suppose, can testify what arms the bedells' staff hath upon them, for he is stationer to the university.

He hated the university with a hatred born of personal experiences; when he, an Oxford man of sorts, could actually suggest to Cromwell that the university, not being incorporated, had no right to all the liberties it claimed, the town possibly having a better title on occasion, apostasy could go no further.

By way of winding up, the paper turns to the bishops, perhaps because Parkins had just complained about the way in which some bishops, founders of colleges, had reserved scholars' places for the shires where they themselves had property and connections, simply in order to keep their lands going – 'impietas pessima'. How they achieved this end by this means is not clear, but Parkins is often confused and confusing. As to the bishops themselves, he makes the practical suggestion that their property be confiscated and they be paid a stipend, but also the Parkinsian observation that at their consecration they have the Holy Scriptures placed on their backs (actually, on their necks), whereas they ought to have them before their eyes 'to look on'.

> And the presumptuous, ambitious, vainglorious, and temerarious bishop of Rome, their extort master, at certain times when he celebrates the holy mass (which I do think is very seldom) standeth upon a book of the Holy Evangel of Christ (*o temeraria audacitas*) (O blessed Jesu) my heart sobbeth at it, etc.

Returning to the point, he arranges for the use of the episcopal revenues: there is to be an almshouse and a grammar school in every diocese, the latter 'for the education of poor men's children'. The king is to have all unnecessary plate and the first fruits and tenths. These last the king had had by statute since 1534. Similar arrangements are made for the abbots and abbesses of monastic institutions as yet undissolved. As for archdeacons, deans, prebendaries and masters of hospitals, there are many enjoying these places who are not priests and some are even children: for them he orders the same treatment, 'mutatis mutandis'. Lastly, he touches on a point which once again reveals him as inclined to reform in religion:

> percase some will say that such manner of men may have no wives; to that may be answered that it is not against Holy Scripture priests to have wives. It is written in Holy Scripture, *quod Episcopus sit unius uxoris vir*, and *preceptum non habeo de virg'* etc., and *Bonum est mulierem non tangere sed melius muliere quam viri*,

the last, in muddled Latin, being apparently a hint of that standard suspicion that celibates practise perversion.

This, then, was John Parkins – a practising lawyer who seems at some time to have suffered a sad interruption to a prosperous career at the bar, author of a textbook not really successful until after his death, an eager dabbler in public affairs, hostile to the university of Oxford, hostile to all priests, in favour of a somewhat uncertain advance towards reform and clearly a passionate student of the Bible, a man of some real ability, some penetratingly critical views and some very wild notions, and one who showed signs of a genuine mental instability. This last shoots through his long paper – his 'rude book' – even if it was written, as he assured Cromwell, 'with great speed and celerity, for on Saturday night last past there was never a word written of it'. The impression he leaves is a mixed one: even at this stage, before we have seen him in action, we cannot help feeling repelled at his eagerness to slander, impressed by his flashes of brilliance, and worried by his obviously failing control.

The men he accused are much less interesting. The abbot of Eynsham (an Oxford monastery) was Anthony

Dunstone, alias Kitchen, who had been elected in May 1530.[9] Cromwell's visitor allowed him chastity, but thought that his failings as a disciplinarian were responsible for the generally bad state of his house. He never showed the slightest desire to resist the Henrician Reformation, subscribing to the royal supremacy in August 1534 and surrendering his house on request in December 1539. His complaisance paid off: in 1545 he was appointed bishop of Llandaff and retained his place till his death, at the age of eighty-six, in 1563. He had the dubious distinction of being the only one of Mary's bishops to accept the Elizabethan settlement. John Burton, the abbot of Osney, the other Oxford monastery, is more obscure. He was elected in 1524 and died soon after the events now to be described, being succeeded by Robert King whom Cromwell put in to organize the surrender of the abbey.[10] These abbots certainly had not the calibre of such men as the last abbots of Glastonbury or Reading who could only be removed by trumped-up charges of treason; they were rather run of the mill, ready on the whole to do as told. But for that very reason they are significant here, for in a sense they represent precisely those innocent men of little weight who (it is alleged) suffered so freely once an informer took it into his head to persecute them. The man who accused them favoured the new world and had the ear both of the lord privy seal, Cromwell, and the lord admiral, Sir William Fitzwilliam; the men accused were abbots when all abbots were suspect, especially after the troubles in the north. On the standard view one would have thought them obvious and helpless victims. Yet the story of John Parkins' charges worked out very differently.

Towards the end of December 1536 Parkins must have

begun to bombard Cromwell with informations, for on 13 January 1537 the abbot of Osney wrote a precautionary letter to the minister.[11] After thanking Cromwell for his manifold kindnesses of which he would be unable to 'recompense the hundreth part' – in rather more than the common letter-style of the period – the abbot went on:

> I have received lately certain letters comprehending great and fearful threats towards me, being written by a neighbour of mine, which (as I suppose) either thinketh or looketh for some great authority shortly, or else he would not give me so high threats; which, unless it should be by the king's grace's power, he is full unable to perform or accomplish the same.

If this man had matter to prefer touching the king, the abbot requested that he be made to disclose it to the king's Council; he himself would be 'ready at all times to come to my answer'. He enclosed the threatening letters as evidence, and happily they survive, attached to the file of papers concerning Parkins' case which is now among the records of Star Chamber.[12]

For, of course, the anonymous neighbour was Parkins, and the letters are most revealing. By sending them to Cromwell, the abbot had taken most of Parkins' wind right out of his sails. They show that Parkins had at one time been engaged on legal business for the abbey, had then fallen out with Burton, and had at last turned on him in disappointed spite. The first of them is full of threats and allusions so obscure that it is necessary to quote at length. The polite forms are preserved, but only just.

> Right honourable, my duty premised; in my most hearty wise I do desire your good lordship, for the love

of the base gentlewoman that dined with you with sauce in your little parlour next the old cloister; when you asked of her – 'how say you, am I fat?' with 'musse, me dearie';* she said – 'by the mass, that you be, hem, mumchance, keep your own counsel'; and for the gentleman's sake that had the falling sickness in your new lodging when Doctor Lison, your prior, and I was by: send to me by the bearer hereof a good ambling gelding for my own riding. And as he is of goodness, so it shall be deserved. My lord, I am your lover if it please you so to take me; and if you do not, I must do as I may. I pray you, give the bearer hereof fair words and do not face ne brace the king his grace's subjects with high and terrible words, saying that you would spend £40 to undo them for executing the king his grace's laws. My lord, he that will not permit ne suffer the king's subjects to enjoy the king's laws is not the king's friend.

The detail may be dark but the purport seems dreadfully clear: Parkins was hinting at knowledge dangerous to the abbot and asking blackmail. Whether he remained friends with him or took steps to ruin him depended on Burton. What is more, Parkins seems to have been successful. His next letter adopts a very different tone. He gives hearty thanks for the gelding: 'if he were a thousand times better than he is, it shall be deserved'. Further, he now throws himself fully into doing the abbot's business. He is sending a draft letters patent by the hand of Master Robert Serls, vicar of St Peter in the East, Oxford, whom at this time he describes as 'a wise, discreet and faithful honest man'. Would the abbot please return the patent sealed with the convent seal. Also – and the cloven hoof appears

---

* 'Musse – a term of endearment' (*N.E.D.*).

31

once more – would he forward £100. The purpose is not stated, except that there is a barely comprehensible note in indifferent Latin suggesting Parkins' need, but in any case later evidence makes it plain that the lawyer was simply turning the screw a little tighter. His success over the horse seems to have gone to his head. To point the moral he describes his good intention:

> This afternoon I ride forth to pacify a furious raging fellow concerning the matter your lordship knoweth of . . . Fear you not: thanks be to God, my fortune is such now that he shall not do your lordship one half-penny worth of hurt.

Before Candlemas the abbot would be as glad of letting Parkins have his way 'as ever was bird of daylight after a dark night'. It does look very much as though he had been playing off two parties to a quarrel; he had got his gelding by threats and was now offering to act the honest man – provided another £100 was forthcoming.

But the abbot jibbed, and the third letter reverted to the tone of the first, with threats and wild, though hidden, accusations. Parkins now had his doubts of Serls. He had asked him to deliver certain letters concerning the king's safety (we shall hear more of this), and instead of rushing to do Parkins' bidding the vicar had delayed for two or three hours before coming round, excusing himself on the grounds that he must serve himself before the king. 'I suppose he will prove an arrant traitor'. Then Parkins once more turned on the abbot:

> And you delay the time in hope of a new world by the means of the insurrection made by the rebellious traitors in the north parts etc. Well, I see well, both religious priests and secular priests be linked together

like a chain of iron against our most dread and benign
sovereign lord the king his grace . . . Sir, if you do send
to me as I have written to you before this present fore-
noon, by William Plummer, . . . I will do the best I
can for you. Cause the patent to be written or drawn
yourself, for I will write and draw no more. I tell to you
plain truth: I had rather that you refuse to do it than do
it, for my profit shall be treble the more.

Here the gloves were off: unless the £100 make a rapid
appearance the abbot will be in very serious trouble, and
it is no good his waiting for times to change and monks to
get the upper hand again. Moreover, in view of what was
to happen later, it is interesting to note that Parkins was
at this time under the illusion that he would greatly benefit by turning informer; no doubt he expected a respect-
able reward from the government.

But the abbot was tougher than expected, or else
Parkins' threats carried little conviction. The brief last
letter could only repeat the purport of the third:

My lord, otherwise than I have written to your lordship
it will not be; by the faith of my body I tell you plain
truth. Fare ye well.

John Parkyns

I remit by the bearer hereof your gloves with the 40s.
in it. Now I perceive you love not your own prosperity,
etc. How then should I love or otherwise love it. My
lord, I am no dallier ne trifler: I do use the plain truth
without any feigning or delay. My lord, make merry a
while; it will not be long, etc.

Apparently Burton had thought himself overcharged by
£98 and had thought to put the blackmailer off with a
gesture; but honest John Parkins was not to be bought so

cheaply. He proceeded to invoke the wrath of king and Council upon the miserly abbot: even while Burton got these letters together and wrote his prophylactic appeal to Cromwell, the Council was contemplating the information that the abbots of Eynsham and Osney had uttered treason. The only one of Parkins' delations to survive accuses Serls of refusing to ride to London with letters 'for the king's safeguard' and at Parkins' bidding. Silly in essence and tailing off into incoherence, it well deserves the disgusted endorsement of the filing clerk: 'a fool of Oxford, or thereabouts'.[13]

But while the Council might think Parkins crazy, they could not, in January 1537, afford to ignore the possible existence of two disaffected abbots. Thus, on 18 January, they sent a writ of privy seal to Sir Simon Harcourt, Sir William Barantyne, William Fermour Esquire, John Williams Esquire, William Fleurs (mayor of Oxford), Michael Heath, John Pye, and William Banester.[14] This asked them to examine John Parkins' allegations that the abbots of Eynsham and Osney 'should speak certain words against Us and Our dignity, contrary to the allegiance they ought to bear unto Us'. If the charges were true, the commissioners were so to certify to the king and Council; if false, they were to see Parkins punished at their discretion. Two points arise out of this document. In the first place, the information (however received originally) was put before the king's Council and not handled by Cromwell privately and personally; secondly, the body taking action was the Privy Council and not the court of Star Chamber which would have employed, not a privy seal, but a writ of *dedimus potestatem* under the great seal. This was as it should be: the Star Chamber could not deal with treasons and felonies, whereas the Council as an executive body could, and was bound to, make inquiries into such matters of state. If the commissioners found a *prima facie* case against the abbots and sent them up, the Council would have to arrange for a proper trial either in the King's Bench or more probably before a special commission of *oyer and terminer*.[15]

The commissioners appointed deserve some attention. There was absolutely no question of packing this body so as to weight the balance against the accused; on the contrary, the men chosen were the obvious persons to execute any government commission at Oxford, for they were a mixture of leading gentlemen of the county and borough dignitaries. Harcourt, Barantyne, Fermour, and Williams were all on the commission of the peace for 1536–7.[16] Fleurs was mayor of Oxford; Pye and Banester were aldermen, the latter to hold office as mayor in the following year;[17] from his position in the list, Heath, of whom nothing else is known, may also have been an alderman, though (as we shall see) there is just a chance that he may have been an agent of the government. Furthermore, the leading members of the commission are known to have been at least unsympathetic towards the new order of things. Harcourt, an old man of much influence in the shire, had the reputation of favouring priests and looking askance on men who informed against them,[18] though this did not prevent him from seeking the make profit out of the dissolution of the monasteries.[19] Barantyne, who represented Berkshire in the Reformation Parliament, was one of a group who had incurred some suspicion of unconstitutional faction-making outside the House: he had discussed Parliament matters at the Queen's Head tavern in company with men whom the government was watching with care.[20] On the other hand, in May 1538 the three Oxford aldermen together with Robert King (Burton's successor at Osney) signed a deposition against a priest who had preached purgatory contrary to the Injunctions of that year.[21] This, of course, it was their duty to do. Naturally, the men commissioned to investigate Parkins' allegations were not known enemies to the king and realm, but neither were they creatures of the Council. They were local magistrates – the proper authorities – and far from being fully committed to Cromwell or his policy.

Within four days of the despatch of the privy seal, on Monday, 22nd January, they met in the Guildhall at Oxford and called Parkins to substantiate his charges. Their report to the Council did not go into much detail.[22] Parkins made his case, 'which were very light matters of malice . . . and of none effect concerning the king's dignity nor against their allegiance'. He was then told to put his accusations in writing and to that end was 'sequestered in a chamber by himself, by the space of three hours or more'. The result appeared in two bills which, he said, included all he knew against the abbots. These were read aloud in court and found harmless. The commissioners therefore ordered him to be confined in Boccardo, the well-known Oxford prison, for the night and next day to be exhibited at Carfax with a paper saying 'for false accusation'; he was then to ask the abbots' forgiveness and remain in prison until Saturday the 27th. 'And forasmuch as the untruth, craft, and subtlety is known of the said Parkins, not alonely in this matter but in many other', it was decided to put him in the pillory at Carfax for one hour if he should still be found in the town or shire of Oxford on 3rd February. It is obvious that the magistrates gladly availed themselves of this opportunity to banish a notorious troublemaker from their jurisdiction.

Though this official account seems to be correct in

essentials, it compresses unduly and leaves a good deal
unsaid. Parkins later described the examination in some
detail to Cromwell, as might be expected with a good deal
more colour.[23] As he came to the Guildhall, one Richard
Cripps, another fellow of the Inner Temple, taunted him
in an attempt to 'deface' him (make him look silly), but
Parkins silenced his jeers by asking whether he were retained as counsel in the case and, on his denying this,
remarking that in the circumstances he had better keep
quiet and let the commissioners get on with the business.
One of these – a man in a coat 'of the new colour' and
with a gold chain, whom Parkins did not know but had
since seen at the Rolls in London, wearing a gown of
'tawny camlet double guarded with black velvet' – then
tried to catch Parkins out on a point of law but was put
in his place. Who this dressy gentleman was is not clear.
Of the commissioners Parkins mentioned Harcourt and
Barantyne by name and is likely to have been familiar
with the Oxford mayor and aldermen, while Fermour was
absent. This leaves Williams, a local gentleman, and the
obscure Heath who perhaps looks the more likely candi-
date. The gentleman's presence at one of Cromwell's
London houses just conceivably suggests some connection
with the government. But all sorts of people crowded
round the Rolls House while Cromwell resided there, and
not too much must be made of it. After this man's retire-
ment from the fray, Harcourt and Barantyne took a hand
in trying to shake Parkins' composure; when they, too,
failed, they at last had the commission read aloud to open
the proceedings. Serls was asked to give his version of
events, and when Parkins interrupted to point out his lies
the vicar turned to the onlookers and laughed 'with apert
risible countenance'. The 'multitude', among whom were
many monks, priests and scholars, joined him heartily.

When Parkins in turn came to put his case, the commissioners 'did even more check and taunt me'. They showed great favour and respect to the abbots, calling them lords 'at every word'. The gentleman in the special coat told Parkins that he was to give his charges both by word of mouth and in writing, whereat he protested that they 'went about *capere me in sermone*' and were untrue to the office of a judge who should be impartial. Clearly Parkins behaved aggravatingly; small wonder that, as he says pathetically, 'they were all against me and as partial of the abbots as though they had been retained with them'. He alleged that the commissioners had their food and drink at the abbots' expense and were dining with them at Fleurs' house. They were there attended by others equally linked with the two monasteries, like Master Fallowfield whose daughter married a servant of the abbot of Eynsham, and Richard Gunter, one of his retainers.

Anyway, Parkins was ordered to go to some house in order to write out his accusations; on the way there the press of priests mobbed him and he had 'three knocks over and upon the reins of my back with the elbows of some of the priests, for the which I shall be the worse during my natural life'. What rankled especially was the fact that he was kept 'under lock and key' while the commissioners and abbots 'were merry together at dinner': it is certainly true that from the first they seem to have treated him as the accused rather than the accuser. After dinner the sitting was resumed in the Guildhall, whereupon Cripps was told to read out Parkins' first deposition in which he recited alleged treasonable talk between the abbots at Eynsham Ferry. To Parkins' disgust, Cripps left out the 'most effectual word', namely 'tush'. Parkins protested and was told to read the paper himself, but at the end they could only say, 'it was but a brabbling [specious] matter'.

In his letter Parkins pointed out indignantly that the self-same brabbling matter had seemed sufficient to the Council to require investigation. As for the question of malice, also alleged against him, surely that made no difference one way or the other as long as his charges were true. That nameless commissioner in the new-coloured coat expressed his wonderment at Parkins' writing to the abbot for £100 by way of a fee (and for another £50 in money of which there is nothing in the extant letters); so Parkins demanded that both parties put in the letters they had exchanged on this subject, which being done ('with much business') allegedly showed the reason for his asking so much. Parkins felt sure that Cromwell had seen the correspondence and agreed with him; we, who have read only the lawyer's letters, could not be sure but were bound to feel rather as the well-dressed commissioner did.

Parkins then deviated into some asides. Burton was guilty not only in the matters alleged, but also 'of buggery, if an indifferent trial might be had'; while Dunstone of Eynsham was also to be charged with the matter concerning Sir Thomas Elyot. This obscure allusion is only partially illuminated by an earlier letter from Parkins to Cromwell, written on 21 January 1537.[24] In this Parkins remembered how the 'vainglorious' abbot of Eynsham had told him a story of Cromwell entertaining Elyot to supper and bidding the author of the *Governour* not to be superstitious – he (Cromwell) was not wedded to abbots. Parkins hinted that both Dunstone and Elyot were papists: the abbot had related how Sir Thomas told him that the emperor of Germany never spoke of the pope without uncovering, and Elyot specially went a mile out of his way to confer with a Dr Holyman, parson at Harborough (Warw.?), under the transparent pretence of a friendly drink, which Holyman was a well-known favourer of the pope. Presumably Parkins dished this stuff up before the commissioners, who can be excused for thinking 'that it was of no value'. The proceedings now deteriorated. A Master Worth (who held a £20 annuity from Eynsham) asked what the abbots' punishment would be if Parkins had his way, and being told that they were liable to suffer death demanded the same for Parkins since he had so falsely accused them. Dunstone himself revived the story of Parkins' *bouleversement* in West-minster Hall, even producing a witness; while Parkins tried to assert himself by showing a letter from Fitz-william, sent with the consent of Cromwell and Lord Chancellor Audley, in which he was apparently asked for details of his denunciations – but the commissioners paid no attention.

At the same time it appears that the commissioners' patience was not yet at an end; they decided to give Parkins one more chance of making good his accusations. He was sent off to the house of Bailiff Pratt to spend the night there in ward and compose a second paper. On his way he was assailed by angry shouts demanding that his ears be cut off and he be put in the pillory. It seems that attempts were made to get him to retract his charges: he was 'craftily handled to speak or to consent to treason'. Yet he was among friends of a sort: after he had gone to bed one of Pratt's servants asked him if he 'would have a fair wench', to which he replied indignantly that the man could 'send all such to the friars, for they be idle persons'. In the morning he composed his second deposition, but the commissioners were by now getting tired of the whole affair. When all had once more assembled in the Guild-hall, Parkins immediately spoke up to demand his rights by the law, but Barantyne remarked that 'I was not well in my mind'. This caused him at last to be silent, though

'my most singular good lord, I thought that the commissioners were not well in their minds' because they so
glaringly ignored the clear tenor of the statutes. Barantyne
said to Dunstone: 'My lord, you may be glad, for your
lordship hath here as fair a day as any man ever had' – yet
against Parkins' asseverations there stood neither proof nor
trial, but only the abbots' mere denial. Parkins pointed out
to Cromwell that 'in all laws' the affirmative is taken for
truth until the contrary be proved, which would indeed
seem to have been sound sixteenth-century doctrine. Then
Barantyne pronounced the sentence which has already
been given; Parkins' version shows that he was to be
exhibited at Carfax on market day, so as to get a good
audience for his showing-up, but only for a quarter of an
hour. He says that during his time in prison more
attempts were made to get him to speak or consent to
treason; also, in a small house (cell?) with but a charcoal
fire to warm him, he was nearly smothered with smoke.
His letter ends with an impassioned assertion that he
spoke the truth and had been very sadly mishandled: he
begs to be restored to his rights and reputation, and to
have his servant released who was yet in prison at Oxford.

Of course, Parkins did not give an impartial account,
but it is obvious even from the commissioners' own return
that what ought to have been an investigation into charges
of treason was immediately turned into the virtual trial of
the accuser. Yet while this is true, and while we may believe that the abbots were treated with marked respect and
deference, it also appears that the commissioners gave
Parkins every chance to make his case. They had no love
for this troublemaker and no doubt liked him no better
for his self-righteous pertness at the opening of the examination, but being commissioned by the Council to
investigate they had to give him a full hearing. After all,

what matters most is not the treatment meted out to John Parkins, hostile though it was when it should not have been, but whether the commissioners protected the abbots against serious and convincing charges of treasonable conversation or had merely to dispose of frivolous and stupid accusations. The evidence is contained in the two depositions which Parkins drew up (in his own abominable handwriting in which so many documents in this case are unhappily written) during the commission's hearings, and which were very properly forwarded together with the commissioners' certificate.

The first deposition tells the story of Parkins' attempts to send information to the Council.[25] On a Thursday morning he sent for Serls and asked him to provide a messenger to carry letters 'to the king his grace's most honourable Council for the king his grace's safeguard'. Serls obtained the services of one John Huggins who, he told Parkins' 'hostess' (landlady), 'would be ready by and by'. After a bit, Huggins knocked at the door of Parkins' lodging; Parkins, in his chamber above the door, called out to know if he were ready and told him to get on horseback and come back together with Serls. 'And I did see no more of the vicar nor Huggins for the space of three hours afterward'. At last Serls returned alone and they met in the garden where Parkins upbraided him: 'Fie, for shame, vicar, art thou not ashamed to tract [delay] the time so long in the king his grace's affairs and business?' To this Serls replied: 'Tush, by God, I must look to myself before the king.' Not perhaps the best considered of remarks, but hardly treason even by the strict standards of the day; nor can one easily agree with Parkins that the omission of 'tush' made much difference to the tenor of the words. Parkins then, dropping into Latin, 'rem taciter considerabam' and handed his letters over. Yet, says he, all the

vicar's important business was 'nothing else but to compromise a matter in variance between him and one
Hewster', a very light matter to cause him to defer
affairs of state 'and a great token of small favour to his
prince'.

It was at this point that he wrote to Burton, surmising
that Serls would turn out to be an arrant traitor and ex-
pressing his conviction that priests and monks were linked
like an iron chain.[26] Upon this Burton went to visit Dunstone. The two abbots met at Eynsham Ferry, with some
twenty-three attendants 'with swords and bucklers and
other weapons, and so made an unlawful assembly'. This
is the only time we hear of this particular accusation, and
we shall not go far wrong if we remember that Parkins
was a trained lawyer who would know well that any charge
of riot (of which the Council would take particular notice)
required some such form of words; there was nothing else
in it. At the ferry, the vainglorious abbot of Eynsham then
allegedly said: 'How say ye, sirs,' and spoke 'the outrageous words, as the vicar knoweth and can say, if he be
a true man'. The vicar and his servant reported these
words to Parkins that same Saturday night. The words
are not given here, but another document suggests their
import.[27] Serls and three others (John Pakington, Robert
Benet B.D., a monk of Westminster, and Philip Poule,
priest) deposed that no words were spoken 'of men and
money enough' at Eynsham Ferry, but that at Eynsham
Abbey itself, on that 13th January, at dinner, the abbot
remarked: 'I thank God and my prince, I have money
enough to retain learned men to defend me against John
Parkins, for all his law.' It thus looks as though Parkins
was trying to turn a remark directed against himself into
one against the king; in the version he gave (and may very
well have believed to be true) the abbot probably spoke of

having men and money enough to resist the king. That the harmless version is correct emerges from the fact that Serls carried the tale back to Parkins, a thing one can imagine him doing if Parkins was the target but not if the words were treasonable.

To return to the story of the letters: in the afternoon of this Saturday Parkins, giving up hope of Serls, met a Master Carter by appointment in the 'new park'. At Parkins' request, Carter sent the lawyer's servant as from himself to the mayor of Oxford, 'and bade him make him ready to ride in all haste' to the Council, to which abrupt request Fleurs naturally returned a dusty answer: 'he could not ne would not ride that night'. This little passage explains a good deal about John Parkins and his reputation in Oxford, and it causes no wonder to find the mayor hostile at the trial. At the time, Parkins said to Carter, 'I marvel at this.' 'By God,' said Carter, remembering, 'William Plummer's daughter shall be married tomorrow, and on Monday, I will warrant you, he shall go.' 'Marry,' replied Parkins sadly, 'thus we may tract the time too long in prejudice of our prince.' But Carter re-assured him: 'No, I warrant you, there shall be no hurt for so long.' So he left the letters (which he now says concerned 'the vicar's crime toward the king his regal majesty' – what crime?) with Carter whom he also asked for a piece of brawn.

However, he had not taken kindly to Carter's heartiness, despite the brawn: 'when he went out of the gate at New Park corner, I bade the devil go with him.' Once more he changed his mind and reverted to his reliance on Serls, the very man he was accusing. He sent the vicar's servant to get the letters back from Carter, intending to send them up faster than Carter seemed prepared to speed them, and early on Sunday he himself took to Serls

the information against the abbots which he had written
out the night before. But when he called at the vicarage he
was left to stand in the open for half an hour, on a cold
frosty morning, 'till that my teeth chattered in my head,
so that I am the worse for it yet and shall be while I live'.
He left the letters, but soon after he got back to his lodg-
ings Serls turned up in some wrath, declaring that the
letters were all lies. Parkins, sick now in his chamber with
the chilling he had had, refused to say another word to
him, but took the letters back and once more sent them
to the mayor. So in the afternoon Fleurs took steps to deal
with Parkins by ordering a body of bailiffs, constables and
others to teach him a lesson – or so we may read between
the lines of Parkins' account. Among these there were
Gunter and Fallowfield, closely associated with Eynsham
Abbey, whom we have already met, as well as one Wapps
who was in the abbot's confidence. They went to the house
of Edward Butter to borrow a candle (though it was
'broad daylight') and proceeded to search some rooms in
Parkins' lodging while he was asleep in his bed. He woke
to a great noise and disturbance in the house, and then the
gang broke in on him. Fallowfield swore 'by the mass, he
would have me to the mayor'. Yielding to force, he went
with them, and at the mayor's door met one Parrott, receiver of Magdalen College, who put 'his face flat against
me to deface me'; and how he behaved himself there let
them testify, and all he has said is true, he will abide by it
'usque ad mortem'.

Thus or something like it, runs his tale; for it is by no
means easy to make sense of Parkins' confused account.
He was clearly under considerable stress while writing.
But what is there in it? Those poor letters of his, embodying some of the information he was sending to the Council, seem to have done a great deal of travelling in Oxford

without ever getting nearer their proper destination, but while it is true that he found it unexpectedly difficult to get them taken to London, it is not clear either that their contents were true, or that (if true) there was treason involved, or for that matter that all the delays were wilful. The most serious accusation – one might say, the only specific accusation – he very probably twisted to his purpose. The deposition tells much more of Parkins and his state of mind than it does of treason and criminal negligence, and the commissioners had every reason for setting it aside as 'a brabbling matter'.

The second deposition suffers from the disadvantage of being an afterthought.[28] As Parkins put it, 'reckoning many diverse and sundry things in my mind this night after my first sleep', further matters were 'infused into my memory'. He recalled an occasion when he called on the abbot of Eynsham, meeting him at the gate of his orchard. As he remembered, it was a fish-day. The abbot sent his attendants to drink with the abbot of Osney's servant who had arrived with a message, and said to his visitor: 'Come on, Master Parkins, you and I will go, talk and see.' After they had walked about the orchard for a little while, the abbot went on: 'Sir, this it is, the abbot of Osney has sent his servant hither with the king's commission that the abbot of Osney and other should sit concerning the lease of my waters to Thomas Fisher.' It appears that Dunstone had been involved in a legal dispute over fishing rights, that a commission of enquiry headed by the abbot of Osney had been appointed (probably by Chancery) and that he was now seeking legal advice from Parkins. The lawyer told him that the commissioners were showing themselves most friendly in thus giving him advance notice. But Dunstone took a very different view: perhaps his case over the fishing rights

would not have stood much looking into. He burst out
that he was a better man than any of them: 'I had rather
they were hanged than I would come before them.'
Parkins gently warned him not to disobey the king's commission or he would undo himself; 'for the passion of
God', he repeated, 'good my lord, do not disobey the king
his grace's commission'. At this the abbot grew very
angry: 'Well, I see well now, thou art not my friend', and
in a fume went off in the direction of the monastry. Parkins continued to pace the orchard for half an hour, until
the abbot again sent for him. He found Dunstone sitting
under the elm in the 'quadrant', surrounded by a crowd of
attendants among whom there stood also Burton's servant
who seemed to have been through the mill a bit, for he
was weeping. As he caught sight of Parkins he ran up to
him and complained that the commission had been
forcibly taken from him, but he got only the unfeeling
reply: 'In good faith, thou art to blame, for thou knowing
me mightst have come to me, and for thy old master's
sake – Master Walbeiff, whose soul God pardon – and
for the abbot of Osney's sake I would have gone with thee
myself and have done thy message to my lord of Eynsham.' As for what became of the king's commission,
'God knoweth and not I.' Parkins really seems to have
been possessed by an irresistible meddling itch, but he
had not proved much with this tale: the abbot may have
been angry about the commission and even spoken as
alleged, in which case he was certainly throwing caution
to the winds, but clearly Parkins could not show that he
had in fact contemned the king's seal by refusing to
appear before the commission.

His night-thoughts dredged up a few more damaging
details. The abbot of Eynsham had (he said) frequently
stated 'in a fumish raging fashion': 'Na, na, I will be

content to hear the king his grace's laws but will not do after them.' Perhaps Dunstone really was the sort of bore who would make a habit of such a phrase and think it funny. Also – and here perhaps we have the source of Parkins' spleen – the abbot had asked allowance in the Exchequer for a patent (probably an annuity) held by Parkins, and yet the lawyer had never had a penny. Also, 'it is very like' that the abbot was deceiving the king as to the revenues of his abbey when it came to the assessment of the annual tenth – a thing very unlikely indeed, for the tenth was levied in accordance with the valuation recorded, in 1535, in the *Valor Ecclesiasticus* which was based on a thorough and efficient investigation. That is all he can think of, and he again appeals to God to save the king and swears to the truth of his saying.

There is no need to labour the point: on this evidence no one would hang a dog, or even an abbot in the year of the pilgrimage of grace. When Parkins sent delations to Cromwell and the Council they were bound to look into the matter, and they did the proper thing by commissioning local magistrates to investigate. But the magistrates were patently right in throwing the charge out, though quite probably they displayed rather more animus against the informer than went well with judicial impartiality. Possibly this story cannot succeed in destroying the view that innocent men, accused lightly and falsely of speaking treason, suffered dreadful things from a ruthless and evil government: perhaps no single story can dispose of so vast and so glib a generalization. But the generalization has never before been put to the test, and in this instance, when this was done, it fell down completely. Those, on the other hand, who have believed and publicized the hostile view of Cromwell's government have never thought it necessary to provide any evidence at all for the particular charge that any delation was likely to take a man to the scaffold.

In the original privy seal the government had ordered the commissioners to deal with Parkins as they thought fit if he should be found untrustworthy, and they intended to exhibit him publicly, make him apologize and keep him in Boccardo for a few days. Distressed the prisoner was — the treatment cannot have benefited his wavering sanity — but he had some hope left. The day after the investigation closed, on 24th January, he wrote from prison to the lord admiral, reminding him that Fitzwilliam, Cromwell and Audley had wished him to come up to London and tell his story in person. Since then, he said, the privy seal had arrived; and he recited the dire events that had resulted.[29] He appealed for help, and his appeal did not go unheard. By the 28th he could thank Cromwell for a letter which had saved his life.[30] 'O my especial and most singular good lord, I have been tormented for observing my allegiance.' Seemingly Cromwell, though content to accept the commission's findings, inclined to a similar view: it appears from this letter that he had got Parkins out of prison, though he was presumably too late to save him the public humiliation at Carfax. Parkins made the true point that the commission was supposed to examine charges against the abbots and not, as they did, 'matters in variance between the abbot of Osney and me'. But there is no sign that Cromwell would do more than save Parkins from some of the consequences of his own folly and wild temper. He could not stop the lawyer writing letters to him: in this one he also read the scheme for breaking up the northern rebellion (which in any case had been virtually over for some weeks), and soon after he must have received the great plan for reforming the universities and secularizing the Church lands, written in such haste that Parkins three times recurred to it in order to add the Order of St John of Jerusalem and various large vicarages to the organizations he wished to be treated, *mutatis mutandis*, like the monasteries.[31] Cromwell also received the long letter which has provided us with so graphic an account of the proceedings in the Oxford Guildhall.

Exiled from Oxford and apparently in some difficulties, Parkins continued to bombard the lord privy seal with letters of praise and entreaty which, being undated, cannot be well arranged or placed. Complaining that his recent treatment had ruined his good name and his health, he asks for restitution and amends.[32] For a lyrical appeal he drops into Latin: 'In dominacione tua . . . est omnis spes mea. Tua iustitia, O mi domine, eripe me e malis et libera me.' Forever will he praise Cromwell's goodness.[33] The next letter is all in Latin: 'Ego autem mendicus sum et pauper; deprecor maiestatem tuam ut solicitor sis mei. Adiutor et protector meus tu es. Ad adiuvandum me festina.'[34] It is somewhat elementary Latin, but at least, unlike some of his tags, it is grammatical. The appeals seem to have secured some sort of hearing. After a little while Parkins could write thanks to Cromwell for being a good lord to him and promising to see about finding him 'such a mean living' as the minister thought expedient. Parkins – poor and destitute as he claimed to be – offered Cromwell £100 and the prospect of £2,000 if only Cromwell would listen to him;[35] the lord privy seal, allegedly so greedy of bribes, does not appear to have been impressed. Parkins had been counting unhatched chickens: even repeated offers of £100 got him no more than a command to attend on Cromwell for the favour of a private interview.[36] But the fate of poor suitors in the sixteenth century was commonly to wait and watch. Parkins fared likewise.

Obeying the command he attended for day after day, throughout three weeks, until finally he had speech with Cromwell. The comfort he got was less than slender, for Cromwell – with more malice, one feels, than unction – told the importunate man 'to be content to live the mean life'. Parkins expressed himself willing but unable to do even so little unless Cromwell showed him favour; he asked for the mastership of the Savoy. The present master did not deserve the place; apart from his personal shortcomings he had plenty to live on and only seven sisters to maintain, not thirteen as he claimed.[37]

As far as is known, Parkins was never successful in this suit, though he must have obtained some sort of living for the eight years remaining to him. Cromwell clearly took his measure and thought him unworthy of more than a tiny favour. At the same time these last letters are much less distraught than the earlier ones. Perhaps, after all, the 'fool of Oxford' managed to settle down without serious mental derangement. He had got himself into bad trouble through his meddling self-importance and his quarrelsomeness. Cromwell had listened to his accusations and thought it right to get him out of gaol when these proved worthless. He had neither simply taken the informer's word and destroyed innocent men, nor been prepared to look kindly upon a man who had tried to start a witch-hunt. Possibly unprovided, certainly fallen from his station, John Parkins lived on, to die in 1545. His book survived him, a memorial of the sharp brain and professional skill of his better days.

2

CAMBRIDGE RIOTS

An academic story

The early sixteenth century was a time of much trouble and quarrelling between the town and the university of Cambridge. Cooper's *Annals* and various volumes of records recite one set of articles after another in which the mayor and burgesses charged the vicechancellor, his proctors, and scholars with breaches of the peace and usurpation of power; on the other side, the university often felt its ancient privileges in danger and attempted to secure fresh recognition from king and Council. How unquiet a time it was is illustrated with pungency by the diarist who recorded in 1534 that

> that same night was parson Yaxley drinking at the Angel until nine o'clock, and in going from thence to the Dolphin about the back door of Burden Hostel he lost his gown and his tippet. And the next night after, there was stripes given betwixt Master Alyson of the King's Hall and Symson, and either hurt the other with daggers very sore.[1]

The pub-crawling cleric presumably has only himself to blame for his somewhat disconcerting losses, but the gentlemen of King's Hall who used daggers to settle their quarrels in a fashion which would enliven some present-day donnish controversies gave proof of an unusual vigour. Scholars who would fight each other after dark and stick knives in each other's ribs were not likely to hang back when the cry of privileges endangered was raised against the townspeople.

The common causes of quarrels were two: rival police jurisdiction, especially since the mayor and the vice-chancellor each justifiably suspected the other of bearing favour in cases which involved both burgesses and scholars; and the control of victuallers and markets— more particularly of Stourbridge Fair – which was profitable to the authorities and vital to both the town folk and the members of the university. In 1503, Lady Margaret Beaufort brought the parties to arbitration, but the settlement then arrived at – which was very full and long and detailed – served little purpose beyond acting as a touchstone in the continuing quarrels which it could not prevent.[2] Moreover, it seems likely that traders of various kinds tried to exploit the jealousies of the licensing authorities in order to reduce the fees they had to pay, so that their constant playing off of one against the other kept the fires going. Both these matters – affrays and market jurisdiction – animated the troubles of 1533–4 of which for once a little more is known since both parties bombarded the court of Star Chamber with bills and answers. Unfortunately, all Star Chamber degrees being lost, we have no idea what the council decided and shall not find it easy to arrive at the truth; what we have to go on are some lengthy but regrettably uninformative witnesses' depositions and some voluble but distinctly *ex parte* statements from plaintiffs and defendants. However, eked out with one or two other records, these should be enough to reconstruct the events of July 1533, and of February and April 1534, when the smouldering embers burst into flame.

For the first of these occasions we have to rely on one bill of complaint put in jointly by two of the accusers – William Gyll, an ex-mayor of Cambridge, and John Chapman, alderman and miller[3] – and on another bill from Robert Chapman, mayor of Cambridge in 1534;[4] there are further some totally useless answers by two of the men whom Robert Chapman accused[5] and some depositions taken by the clerk of the council (Thomas Eden) in reply to Robert Chapman's interrogatory.[6] The plaintiffs alleged that on 16 July 1533, about 11 or 12 o'clock at night, they were attacked in their houses by a mob of scholars and members of the university. They named William Pannell, taxer of the university and fellow of Michaelhouse, Nicholas Gladman and David Whyte, fellows of St John's College, Robert Whytehead, a scholar of Burden's Hostel,* William Payne, a cook of St John's College, and about thirty others. The rioters were armed with swords, bucklers, clubs, daggers and the like, though in assessing this charge it must be borne in mind that such details were common form in a bill since without them the court of Star Chamber would not be competent to try the case. Windows and doors were broken, as well as the sign of Robert Chapman's house (the 'Black Bull'), and there were menaces to 'slay and beat them, with horrible and outrageous shouts'. The mob yelled at Gyll, 'Thou whoreson butcher [which we may suppose he was – a butcher,

---

* A hostel of residence 'near the postern of Wolf's Tavern to the North ward', near the present Trinity Lane, which belonged to Clare but before that to St John's ([Richard Parker], *History and Antiquities of the University of Cambridge*, 1721, p. 31. The author of this work, a fellow of Caius, died in 1624: *ibid.*, p. 26).

that is], we would that we had thy butcher's head here'; and at both Chapmans, 'Thou arrant whoreson, we shall teach thee to keep a good tongue in thy head'; and there was more of this sort of refined academic reproof.

For good measure, Robert Chapman added that William Doughty, vicar of Caldecote (a village a few miles east of Cambridge), John Coverdale of St Nicholas' Hostel* and vicar of Haslingfield (a village to the south-west), Edmund Davy of St. John's, and several other gownsmen had raised similar riots on three earlier occasions, namely about All Saints' Day 1531, Christmas Day 1532 and 7 March 1533 (Friday in Ember Week). On this occasion in July 1533, the sudden disturbance sadly upset all three men, their wives and children and servants, driving some of them 'almost out of their wits'; since that day they had continued in such fear of their lives that they dared not go out after dark themselves or send their servants on errands. This last picturesque detail may well raise doubts, for there is good reason to suppose that this bill was drawn up some six or eight months after the events complained of, during which time Gyll and the Chapmans will hardly have undergone this sort of all-night house arrest. The readiness with which suitors in Star Chamber represented themselves as miserable cravens shivering in every breeze and meriting the authorities' compassion rather than justice, is – incidentally – an interesting sign of a change in values that has certainly taken place since those days. Gyll and his fellows took the proper steps: they had the rioters indicted at the next sessions (which do not appear to have taken place until December) before the justices of the peace for the borough. This in no way intimidated the bullies who talked at large

* *Ibid.*, p. 31: 'The Houses opposite to the House now call'd *Brazen George*, near Christ's College.'

about what they would do to the jury which had found a true bill against them, saying that they 'had been better to have been a thousand miles thence'. Altogether, the complainants alleged a reign of terror in Cambridge; the town officers had been too afraid to keep a proper watch at night, so that several suspected felons and vagabonds had passed through without hindrance. Undoubtedly it was felt that this last point would make the Council sit up: it affected government policy and interests.

We can modify this highly-coloured account only by the use of common sense; the other side is not on record. Those of the accused whose replies to the interrogatory are preserved spoke with a great air of conscious rectitude and surprise at such charges. Pannell, the taxer, could not understand why his old friend Robert Chapman should have thus turned against him; he had no knowledge of any doings on the fatal night, the more so as he was then preparing himself for a journey to London on university business, a journey on which in fact he started next morning. A suspicious mind might see a sinister significance in this well-timed departure. He had to account for the presence of a 'harness' (some bits of military equipment) in his chamber, a serious matter since it could be used to prove armed rioting, but he did so by saying that Master Take, then senior proctor, gave it to him on the preceding 10th of April when he was asked to assist in searching 'for certain evil-disposed women, to see them corrected and punished for their lewdness'. No one was more surprised than Master Pannell when he was told on Christmas Eve that he stood indicted of rioting, and he denied all the charges with vehemence. Edmund Davy had no idea how Chapman's windows and door came to be broken; he never 'went a-getting', except with the proctor. To go a-getting was the technical term for raising a band for law-enforcement or for rioting – according as you looked at it. Davy admitted being mixed up with a mob on the fatal day, but as far as he was concerned it was all very innocent. A certain priest, Sir Nicholas Williams of Bourn in Cambridgeshire, who happened to be visiting Cambridge that day and was putting up 'at the sign of the Horn', asked Nicholas Gladman to have a drink with him, and Gladman asked Davy along as well. They decided to have a pint at the Round Tavern, but on their way 'there came getters to them and there drove them in again into the said inn of the Horn'. And that was all he knew.

William Doughty, on the other hand, admitted that he and Chapman had been enemies for fifteen years and also produced a reason for the riot. Apparently it was rumoured that Chapman (who represented Cambridge in the Reformation Parliament)[7] was sponsoring a bill in Parliament to diminish the liberties of the universities. If such tales were told, it is indeed little wonder that windows were broken. Doughty himself, like John Coverdale and the redoubtable cook of St. John's College (whom we shall meet again) were, of course, quite innocent, had taken part in nothing and knew nothing of the instigators of the riot. Coverdale could not imagine why poor Chapman, whom he had known as an honest man for twelve years, should have been so ill-treated. What the Council made of these stories we do not know; probably little enough, for they were used to trouble at Cambridge and soon found themselves confronted with more serious examples of it.

For the riots of February 1534 we have both sides of the case stated, though this will not necessarily make it easier to establish the truth. The university was forced by its opponents' action to put in a bill many months after the event.[8] This began with a rehearsal of ancient privileges – cognisance of pleas involving scholars of the university unless they concerned felony or mayhem, and the right to hold the assize of bread, ale, wine and other victuals both at Cambridge and at Stourbridge Fair, as well as the oversight of weights and measures. In order to illustrate the danger to the first, the bill referred to the assaults made by John Jenynges, husbandman, Hugh Hare, labourer, and [Richard] Colynson, labourer, upon scholars and their servants. The description of these men was, as we shall see, a trifle contemptuous – no doubt designedly so. What happened is described more fully in the diary of John Mere, bedell and later registrary of the university:[9]

> Upon Candlemas Day [2 February 1534] the proctors' servants, with Master Whyte, Gladman and S: Greene, went to the castle end to seek a drab, where bailiff Jenynges and Hare with diverse others set upon them. . . .

Naturally, a minor battle developed. Jenynges and Hare were, then, the bailiffs of the town and not mere labourers. The proctors' constant activity in searching the town for prostitutes is perhaps a little surprising, even though no doubt it arose from their proper solicitude for the young men in their charge; it is not unlikely that—as in the case of Pannell before—this was the standard story to tell when a crowd had gone out looking for trouble. Who started it is not clear so far; Mere concludes by saying that 'on the morrow after, Jenynges and Hare rode to London to complain of the proctors and their servants'.

Indeed they did, and the tale they told was a very different one;[10] for simplicity's sake it had best be related as though it were simple fact. On 2 February 1534,

Hare, with his wife and children, was peacefully at his home in St Peter's parish, Cambridge. About 6 or 7 o'clock in the evening, the house was surrounded by Edmund Davy, Nicholas Gladman, William Payne and some ten or more other 'riotous and misruled persons' who attacked 'with swords, bucklers, daggers, clubs and staves and other defensive and invasive weapons and habiliments of war'. They proceeded to 'sore hurt and beat' poor Hare and to throw Richard Colynson on a bed in the house, 'and there would have sticked him with a dagger' but that help came. From Hare's chamber they took a paper which he had brought according to the king's commandment; what this was he does not tell us. Later, about eight, the rioters broke into Jenynges' house and upon his return home attacked and beat him; he would have been killed if Hare and other neighbours had not come to the rescue. After drawing off, they came again to Jenynges' place about midnight and created a rumpus; there were cries of 'down with the doors' and 'fire the house', so that Jenynges for sheer fear opened up. This time the mob was led by the senior proctor himself, no less a person than Nicholas Ridley, who took it upon himself to make a search of the house, though to what purpose Jenynges said he did not know. Having finished with Jenynges – and there seems to have been no assault this time – the rioters, with Ridley still at their head, pressed on to Hare's house, demanding admittance in the same vigorous manner. But Hare seems to have thought his chances even worse than those of Jenynges; afraid to face the crowd, he fled 'at a back gate, barefoot and bare-legged', running two full miles to Coton village where he 'was fain to borrow a pair of hosen' from an acquaintance, 'which hosen your said suppliant yet weareth'. He alleged that he had not dared to go home since; if Mere is to be trusted, this was in part at least because he had gone to London (in his borrowed hosen, one supposes) to pursue his suit before the Council.

A certain amount of either version of the tale will, of course, have to be disallowed: it is to be feared that Hare and Jenynges may have exaggerated, and Mere may not (it is possible) have told the whole truth. At the same time, it would have been a pity indeed if these respective stories had never been written down. Looking at the matter with such absence of passion as 400 years may cause to supervene, one feels justified in supposing that Hare and Jenynges, apparently well known as leaders of town against gown, had engaged in a free-for-all with the proctors' party on Castle Hill in the afternoon of February 2nd. Incensed by this, those ardent spirits – Davy, Gladman and Payne (St John's to the fore, it would seem) – gathered a band in the evening to teach the two bailiffs a lesson. Quite possibly the paper taken from Hare's house concerned the attempts then being made by the town to reduce the university's privileges; since these attempts were of dubious justice, Hare's slurring over the precise nature of the 'bill' would be explained. The interpretation would also account for the later midnight descent with the proctor himself in charge – eager, we may guess, to scotch any attack on the rights it was his duty and pleasure to maintain and enforce. I suspect that no one suffered much bodily discomfort, unless Hare really did those two miles to Coton on his bare feet with his shirt tails flapping in the February night air. I cannot believe, on the evidence, that there was much danger of killing, though Colynson – flung on his back and tickled with a knife – and Jenynges – ambushed and beaten up in his own house – might well disagree with such an unasked-for opinion. What is certain is that no one was actually killed: we should for sure have heard about that. But it was a lively night.

The sequel, inconclusive though it was, is less in doubt. First of all, there was another little incident on the night of Shrove Tuesday (17th February) when a band of about thirty 'getters' made proclamation on Market Hill and 'there asked a banns between Shevelling Ralph of the Bell and a burnt whore of Jesus Lane'. This has the air of an undergraduate rag of the more elementary kind. To call the banns between a tapster and a streetwalker might appeal to riotous young men even today as a capital joke. Having had their fun, they went on to chase poor Dr Buckmaster, master of King's Hall and the vice-chancellor's deputy, through the streets; Mere, employing a telling metaphor, says they 'coursed' him. The miserable hare beat the hounds to it; he slipped into King's Hall and shut the gates and then called them knaves through the bars; to which they replied that 'if they had him without, they would make him a knave'. After these amenities, peace seems to have returned.[11]

But this, though it shows something of the temper of sixteenth-century undergraduates, is admittedly a little off the point. As far as the Candlemas riot was concerned, it developed into a quarrel over jurisdiction.[12] Dr Buckmaster, as deputy to the vicechancellor, decided to call before him those townsmen who had attacked the proctor on Castle Hill – for that, of course, was the way he saw it. They appeared on 27th March,[13] but of those present Hare and Jenynges refused outright to admit the vicechancellor's jurisdiction or answer to the charge, while Colynson produced a pretty piece of lawyer's argument. He said he was obviously called either as a witness or as a party; if he was a witness, 'answer was and should be made before a better man and higher judge', while if he

61

was a party he would 'answer before their own head', that is the mayor. He added that the mayor himself – Robert Chapman, the champion of the town's claims – had instructed him to say this. Rather disconcerted and pretending to believe that the mayor could not possibly be behind such contumacy, Buckmaster sent the junior proctor, Richard Wilkes, with Mere, the bedell, and Richard Carter, M.A., to the Guildhall. Chapman blandly told them that he had the duke of Norfolk's pleasure to the effect that the case should be heard by the mayor and vicechancellor jointly. Since Norfolk was high steward of the borough, it is clear that the mayor had been more successful than the vicechancellor in mobilizing his patron, and it must have become very obvious to the university that to be saddled with a chancellor (Bishop Fisher) who was already on his way to the Tower might prove a serious disadvantage. There can be no doubt that by ancient custom, royal grant and the 1503 composition, a case of riot involving townsmen and scholars ought to have been heard by the vicechancellor or his deputy, so that Norfolk's reply greatly favoured the town. Having made his unanswerable point, Chapman drove it home by demonstrating the impossibility of any joint action: it was, he added, manifest in any case that here scholars alone were guilty, as was proved by the attack on Hare's house. With this deadlock the matter ended, as far as we know, except that the university in its bill pointed out plaintively how unfortunate it was that such offences should go unpunished; they hoped the Council would take action. There is nothing to show that it did.

Even while the Candlemas riots were still casting their shadows, the biggest troubles of the year were about to brew up. The riots of 10–18 April 1534 are quite fully documented, but to follow them from bill to answer and through witnesses' depositions would be both tedious and confusing. Instead I shall attempt to reconstruct the events by means of all the material and tell the story connectedly. There is, first, the bill preferred by the mayor, Robert Chapman, against Nicholas Ridley and Richard Wilkes, proctors, and against their servants – John Ridley, John Parker, William Wyntryngham, Robert Legett and Thomas Towy.[14] Next we have the accused men's answer[15] and interrogatories to be administered to them in Chapman's behalf at the suit of the attorney-general;[16] the troubles at Cambridge were being taken sufficiently seriously for the crown to take a hand in clearing them up. The next document in sequence is a writ of *dedimus potestatem*, addressed to Sir Richard Lister, chief baron of the Exchequer, ordering him to swear witnesses to appear before Thomas Eden, clerk of the Council, whom the court of Star Chamber was sending down to Cambridge to take depositions.[17] Lister appears to have been the assize judge that year: Mere's diary mentions a visit which the vicechancellor paid to him, 'the judge', in Cambridge, in connection with the earlier troubles.[18] The chief baron rendered a certificate of the men he had sworn,[19] and Eden's examination – or part of it – also survives.[20] On the basis of all these papers, the story can be told with some confidence that we know what it was about.

On Easter Eve – 4th April – 1534, Robert Chapman, mayor of Cambridge, went into the market-place to see that things were running smoothly. He found instead a scene of some perturbation. People crowded up to him to complain that the butchers were selling their meat at prices above the statutory maximum and that they alleged proctorial permission to do so. Chapman therefore sought out the junior proctor, Richard Wilkes, who was also perambulating the market, to know why this had been done. According to himself, he spoke 'charitably and quietly, to see the king's subjects so indifferently ordered that no grudge or other inconvenience should or might ensue'. The proctors' case was that proclamation had recently been made by the king in Council, permitting butchers to sell meat at half a farthing more per pound than was appointed by the price-fixing act of 1533, thus bringing beef and pork to a halfpenny and half a farthing the pound, and mutton and veal to a halfpenny farthing.[21] Of this proclamation the vicechancellor had been informed by letter, so that the proctors had no hesitation in authorizing the new prices when approached by the butchers who had argued that 'they could not have no convenient living' at the old ones. Since Wilkes, however, had no copy of the proclamation to show, he had to content himself with telling Chapman that 'there was a proclamation made the Wednesday before at Royston in the market there' to the effect stated, and that 'he thought it as lawful to execute the said proclamation in Cambridge as in Royston'. Chapman, allegedly in a great fury, retorted that the proctor 'had done the people the more wrong to cause them to pay higher prices for their said flesh', and also that (if such a proclamation existed) it was his duty and not the proctors' to see it carried out; for by the last act the authority was now committed to the mayor. To this Wilkes merely remarked, according to Chapman: 'I will advise you not to meddle with the said weight of flesh, for if ye do it shall be to your pain.' Upon these threatening words, reinforced as they were by the presence of John Parker looming up behind his master with sword and buckler, the mayor withdrew in fear that 'breach of the king's peace and other inconveniences' might follow. Wilkes, who admitted all the rest, categorically denied ever uttering the threats complained of; he said that the mayor did not leave the market for fear of violence since there was no cause why he should have feared any.

The quarrel was well chosen. It arose out of a matter of vital importance both to the butchers and to all purchasers of meat, that is the whole population of town and university; it spread at once and with characteristic ease into the field of university privileges and rival jurisdictions; and it was based on a serious weakness in the recent legislation concerning food prices. An act of 1533[22] had established maximum prices for meat, permitting certain named officers to lower − though not to raise − them if it seemed desirable. Though mayors of corporate towns were specifically included among these officers, there was also a proviso saving the right of executing the act to 'such person and persons as now have or that hereafter shall have the authority of clerk of the market, or to set price of victuals, within the towns and universities of Oxford and Cambridge'. There was no doubt that the proctors and taxers, acting for the vicechancellor, had always exercised the office of clerk of the market, claiming royal grants and ancient prescription.[23] This the mayor did not attempt to deny. But he could put up a case because in the session just concluded on 30 March 1534 there had been another act passed which, among other things, confirmed the earlier statute but also made some new provisions.[24] It authorized mayors, sheriffs, bailiffs and the like to imprison offenders and do various things, but it failed to make mention of the universities or their officers. Section iv of the act empowered the crown to make temporary alterations in the price of meat by proclamation; the mayor now claimed that by not referring to the rights of Oxford and Cambridge dons in the markets of those towns the act transferred all execution of matters

65

under it to him – and this, of course included the enforcement of royal proclamations. The occasion of the trouble – whether the poor people's inability to pay that half farthing a pound more for their meat, or the poor butchers' inability to make a living unless they did – was quickly forgotten; it does not receive another mention in the story. Instead town and gown settled down to a familiar struggle over university privileges, in this case whether the ancient powers of the vicechancellor as clerk of the market were superseded by the failure to make reference to them in the last relevant statute. It was the sort of point that the courts would have loved to clear up, but the temper of Cambridge undergraduates was less litigious than riotous, and they did not propose to leave the decision to the lawyers.

The intervention of Easter called a truce, but tempers were only the hotter for being kept simmering. By the following Friday fears that Chapman intended to enforce the royal proclamation himself on the following market day overcame such little discretion as was to be found in the university. At four o'clock in the early morning of Saturday, 11th April,* a number of undergraduates – the proctors later denied that they had been privy to the event – set up the following bill on the market cross:

This day the mayor and the freemen of Cambridge purposes to cry and proclaim that no proctor nor taxer shall exercise their office and authority which was granted to them by the most noble and redoubted King Henry and hath so been used the reign of diverse princes; and therefore the university shall make the

* The mayor's bill said 10 April; the interrogatory spoke of 4 a.m. on the 11th. Probably the scholars began to be restive on the Friday, in expectation of the market day on the morrow, but did not take active steps till the early hours of Saturday.

crier thereof to cease both crying and calling for a long day, whatsoever he be depending the town of Cambridge; except he have the king's authority to show for him, which the university trust they cannot purchase of the king's grace, they have such confidence in his goodness.

It was an unequivocal incitement to riot. The chances are that the proctors' denial of complicity was genuine, for the bill seems to have taken them by surprise: about 8 o'clock on Saturday morning they visited the mayor at his house and asked him, in the vicechancellor's name, if it was true that he intended to make proclamation that day. Chapman replied, with the utmost correctness, that he had no command from king and Council and that he would like the vicechancellor to be told that he would make no proclamation until he had such command. 'And with this answer the said proctors departed, as to the said mayor appeared right well contented.'

So far Chapman, under considerable provocation, had behaved very well; unquestionably he was leading on points. But the serious riots of this Saturday's market were largely due to action on his part which bore the marks either of complete folly or of deliberate trouble-making. Round about ten in the morning he had word that John Hynde, serjeant-at-law and recorder of Cambridge, was in the market-place, and he decided to go and talk with him. The two borough dignitaries met at the church door of the Austin Friars, roughly at the corner of Peas Hill and Bene't Street.* By now the market was filled

* The Austin Friars occupied a square of buildings bounded by the modern Peas Hill, Free School Lane, Pembroke Street, and Corn Exchange Street; there were gates opening on Peas Hill (*Victoria County History, Cambridgeshire*, ii. 287 f.).

with members of the university, expecting trouble and ready to follow up the bill posted on the market cross by preventing the town crier from making proclamation concerning the price of meat. Some of them strayed towards Peas Hill and watched the colloquy between mayor and recorder from a distance. Whatever the two may actually have talked about – and Chapman is very vague on this point – the undergraduates naturally suspected the hatching of plots; indeed, it would be surprising if the two men could have avoided talking of these matters while standing less than a hundred yards from a market place seething with excitement. After a time they decided to pay a visit to the market in their official capacity, and they had no sooner moved off than the watchers at the corner ran ahead 'with all the haste that they could devise . . . crying, they come, they come'.

The mayor and the recorder entered the market place in procession, with their maces carried before them; peaceably, Chapman says, and undoubtedly they did not actually start any trouble, but the manner of their appearance, after the lengthy consultation held at the Austin Friars' gate, was not calculated to assuage suspicion. They found the market-place in a state which greatly 'astonished and abashed' them. The proctors appeared to be in virtually military occupation of the middle of the square; allegedly they had left the market earlier, but had returned post-haste as soon as news of the borough officials' approach reached them. They had now taken up their stand, with their attendants, between the stall of John Gaunte, grocer, and the market cross; to Chapman's and Hynde's startled eyes they appeared to be surrounded with an armed band, 'having upon them and about them swords, bucklers and other weapons defensive'. From this centre of opposition, groups of scholars stretched right over to 'Richard Lichfield's corner', an unidentifiable place; but it can be said that Lichfield (who was a vintner as well as acting as grocer, fishmonger and salter) may have provided in his tavern something of a centre for ardent university supporters. He had been in trouble with the borough as early as 1514 when, being bailiff, he had refused to account for certain money and claimed privilege as a servant of the university; the town had resented this the more because Lichfield was a 'foreigner', born in Wood Rising in Norfolk, whom they had kindly made a freeman in 1503.[25] On this 11 April 1534 it would appear that he had many undergraduates drinking at his place, ready to join in the fray when occasion offered. Perhaps his place was the 'Lilypot' which occurs in the later depositions as a tavern occupied by scholars. One witness deposed to seeing about fifty scholars round Lichfield's corner when he himself went to the tavern to drink a pint of wine with a couple of friends; he could add nothing further, 'for he sat in the house drinking till all the said scholars were gone'. Clearly it was possible for a man to abstract himself from the troubles of that day. Many undergraduates were gathered about the market-place in 'bushments and companies', some sitting on fish stalls—to the number of altogether about 200, according to Chapman whose witnesses estimated variously from 100 to 500. At any rate, the market place, busy enough with stallholders and customers, was crammed further with excited young men in scholars' gowns.

The intention of these crowds was not obscure, but much turned on their potential powers for mischief. Were they armed? If they were, they had indeed put themselves in serious jeopardy of the Star Chamber. Chapman naturally claimed to have seen plenty of swords and bucklers and daggers. Equally naturally, Ridley and Wilkes denied these charges and all accusation of riotous assembly to boot. The mayor produced a number of witnesses, but unfortunately for him they proved cagey. No, said one, he saw no weapons, except the swords and bucklers carried by one or two of the proctors' servants. At this time proctorial bulldogs were generally well-advised to follow their risky calling with the help of arms, so that there was nothing much in this. Another witness had heard a rumour of armed bands of scholars in other parts of the town; as for those in the market-place, 'they were in their long gowns and might have weapons under their gowns', but more he could not say. One man saw no weapons at all; another claimed to have seen them under the gowns of about five young men. A husbandman of Dry Drayton had to state that he had not been there at all and only knew what his wife and servant told him who had gone to market that day. And so it went on. Obviously not many weapons were in evidence, whatever the long gowns may have hidden, though a few bits of harness – the odd sword and buckler – could be seen. In all this Chapman's witnesses rather let him down, for he needed the proof of armed preparedness in order to establish his point that he and the recorder had gone in fear of their lives. From the evidence available to us we must say that very likely they were right to fear a beating – one witness deposed that the recorder was 'shouldered' as he entered the market – but that they greatly exaggerated the possibility of murder.

According to Chapman's statement, however, they felt sure that the proctors and scholars intended 'none other thing . . . but utterly to have destroyed and killed the said mayor and recorder in case they had made any proclamation', and their actions were governed by their fears rather than by the reality of a situation which, despite the reservations I have made, was ugly enough. They took one good look at the bands and groups sitting at Lichfield's, on the fishstalls, and gathered round the proctors, and 'for very fear they were fain to forsake and leave their purpose to survey the market and get them to a house'. With sound judgment they picked another of the many wineshops which apparently surrounded the market-place, the house of a certain Hasyll. There they stayed for two hours, leaving the field to the proctors who stood their ground all the time in the middle of the square. This fact seems to have rankled with the mayor and his party, cooped up as they were. They felt that the proctors ought either to have restored order or retired decently; certainly they ought not to have stood there, 'not going about any effectual point or thing touching their office within the said market' and looking with approval upon the antics of their excited followers. Some of these, seeing the mayor and retinue take refuge, were alleged to have given way to threats: 'Well, they be gone now into the tavern; we will advise them to fill their coats well with wine, for surely they shall have upon the coats or [before] they come at home.' The words were denied by the defendants, nor did any of the witnesses admit to hearing them, though they heard much muttering about proclamations.

Then, while the mayor, recorder and mace-bearers sat drinking at Hasyll's and dreading the crowd outside, while Ridley and Wilkes – the church militant – held sway in the market-place, and while some 200 members of the university were milling about waiting for a chance to trounce the infringers of academic privilege – then there came the climax of the day's proceedings. Once again it is difficult to absolve the town from the charge of deliberately provoking an outburst, though the university must bear all the responsibility for taking up the suspected challenge. Into this mob worked up with excitement and expecting at any moment to hear a proclamation read which would go clean contrary to the rights of the university, there came – bravely perhaps but also very foolishly – the town crier. Naturally he had no sooner 'begun to make Oyez', than the houses about the market brought forth numbers of students and there was a concerted rush for the crier. As it happened, he had only got up to make proclamation for a horse that was lost, but at that precise moment no member of the university present but must have thought that the bill put up on the market cross had had the right of it: the mayor was having the proclamation read which it was the vice-chancellor's place to publish. The crier seems to have made his intention understood before anything happened to him, but he had served the mayor's purpose: Chapman now had evidence (as he was not slow to point out) that on that day the making of any proclamation was bound to cause a riot, that the crier would very likely have been killed if his announcement had concerned the university instead of a stray horse, and that the crowd in the market place was in fact assembled to prevent such a proclamation being made. One of the questions he asked to be put to the proctors was whether, on their oath, they could say that, had the mayor made the expected proclamation, 'man-slaughter, fray, riot or other misdemeanour should not have ensued and been committed'; and – on their oath – the proctors could hardly have denied the likelihood. His witnesses, too, supported the mayor in this: nearly all agreed that the crier had been mobbed and that a proclamation concerning the university would have led to 'business and inconvenience', though one man, playing dumb, said dourly that he could not tell why the scholars should have rushed up to the crier, 'except it were to hear the cry'.

On the whole, then, it is fairly certain that the mayor had won the day. Robert Chapman was not the man to retire tamely to a tavern in fear and trembling, unless he had a purpose to serve; he had been in the thick of the riots attending the mayoral election of August 1529 and was clearly something of a firebrand.[26] On this 11 April 1534 he deliberately courted trouble by formally proceeding to a market place filled with his and the town's opponents whom such an entry could only confirm in their suspicions of dirty work afoot against the university's interests. He had then tricked them into showing their hand by sending the town crier to make a totally insignificant announcement. Chapman was not interested in a fight there and then; he wanted material with which to convince the Council in the Star Chamber. The events of the day provided plenty. He rounded off his bill, into which he packed it all, by alleging that on the next market day, a week later, he was again assaulted in the market by the proctors and their adherents, so that he had to leave without doing his duty; the proctors denied this, and Chapman gave neither details nor questions to be asked or witnesses to be examined as he had done in the earlier case, so that very probably this part of the story was invented for good measure. It may be supposed that the proctors, realizing how they had been manœuvred into a false position, managed to restore their control over the extremists among the scholars and to keep the peace on the 18th. But the damage was done, and Chapman could draft his bill to the Council with a pretty good case in hand. Later, in July, John Ridley, a servant and probably a relative of Nicholas Ridley's, one of those named in Chapman's bill,[27] reinforced the case against the proctors

73

by a fracas he had with one Edward Greenberye, servant
to the mayor. According to Chapman, the virtuous Greenberye, obeying strict orders to avoid open conflict,
refused to mix it with Ridley, saying 'Strike me if thou
wilt, for I will draw no knife at thee'; Ridley thereupon
obliged by hitting Greenberye with his dagger. But this
was a minor detail; obviously the case that mattered was
the riot of 11th April which grew out of the perennial
problem of the price of victual in the market and was
immediately developed into a contest over privilege.

Perhaps because at this time the question of the
university's privileges – their extent and confirmation –
was already engaging the Council's attention,* the court
of Star Chamber took up Chapman's bill and pursued
the matter thoroughly. Ridley and Wilkes were required
to make answer to Chapman's accusations, and the university by grace voted them money for their defence.[28]
Later they sent Wilkes and a bedell to London to sue out
a *subpoena* against certain townsmen and to answer the
false accusations of riot 'which was here openly before you
read and lately put up of the foresaid townsmen unto the
king's Council'.[29] But, as has already been said, the
attorney-general himself had taken charge of the matter,

---

* This is a long and complicated story which must not distract us here
at too great a length. It all concerned the running of Stourbridge Fair and
began apparently with some articles prepared by the town to which the
university made answer (Lamb, *Documents illustrative of the History of
the University of Cambridge 1500–1572* [1838], pp. 28 ff.). It ended with
an award in favour of the university made on 25 July 1534 at Lambeth
by Lord Chancellor Audley, Archbishop Cranmer and the duke of
Norfolk (*ibid.* p. 40). In between came lengthy negotiations, the vicechancellor (Simon Heynes, master of Queens' College) spending many
months in London in attempts to engage favour; notes on these matters
may be found in the following places: Cooper, *Annals*, i. 355 ff.; *Grace
Book Γ, 1501–42* (ed. W. G. Searle, 1908), pp. 286 ff.; Lamb, *op. cit.* p. 45.

and the interrogatory to be administered to the proctors
in Chapman's behalf was drawn up by his instructions.[30]
These proceedings produced no result, and it became
necessary to examine the witnesses whom Chapman had
named. Ordinarily the Star Chamber would have commissioned local magistrates to do this, but since in this
case the local magistrates were in fact the contending
parties the court sent its own clerk, Thomas Eden, to
take depositions locally. A writ, dated 23 July 1534 (the
court was acting with unaccustomed speed), instructed
Sir Richard Lister – as already related – to swear certain
inhabitants 'Comitatus nostri Cantebrigiensis ac villarum
eiusdem Comitatus ville nostre Cantebrigiensi adiacien-
tium' to appear before Eden.[31] Lister duly notified Eden
that he had sworn twenty-one men, mostly described as
yeomen, husbandmen or even gentlemen; there were
among them a shoemaker and a butcher, and they
all came from villages near Cambridge – Thriplow,
Rampton, Histon, Barton, Trumpington, Grantchester,
Chesterton, Shelford, Dry Drayton, Girton and Bottisham
– except the cobbler who was a Cambridge man. Chapman
evidently picked his witnesses from people who had visited
Cambridge for the market but might, as outsiders, be
thought the more impartial. Finally, on 2nd September,
Eden got round to taking the depositions at Cambridge,
'by virtue of an order taken by the said Council'; as I have
already had occasion to point out, the witnesses proved
of only doubtful value to the mayor's case. Their answers
are on the whole so carefully guarded and non-committal
as to leave a strong feeling that Eden may have prefaced
his examination with some stern admonitions on the
power of an oath, the admissibility of hearsay evidence
(though some there was), and the need to be sure of the
truth of what was said.

There are no further documents to tell us what was done – whether the Star Chamber in fact decided on the merits of the case or took steps to punish the rioters. But since Nicholas Ridley was involved who is no obscure person, a guess may be permissible. Surely we should have heard about it in some place – surely John Foxe would have told us in his *Acts and Monuments* – if Bishop Ridley had at any time fallen foul of the king's Council and been punished. In this case silence carries a lot of conviction. In the course of 1534 the university succeeded in retrieving part of its fortunes at court, as the negotiations over Stourbridge Fair show; it is not improbable that the rise of Cranmer helped. The chances are that Chapman failed of his purpose, and that no one suffered for the riots of April 1534 when the cry of privilege was raised in the market place at Cambridge, when mayor and recorder suffered the indignity of going in fear of their lives in their own town, and when the town crier could barely announce the loss of a horse without getting his head broken. But it was not until the next year, 1535, that the execution of Bishop Fisher enabled the university to consolidate its position by electing as its chancellor the foremost statesman of the day, Thomas Cromwell, and even Cromwell's influence could not stop the town from pursuing its vendetta. Letter after letter from him to the mayor and borough testifies to this. Time and again in 1535 he addressed them in that tone of dignified, melancholy and marvelling reproof which was as far as Cromwell commonly went in asserting his authority against those who flouted it and to whom he signed himself a loving friend – almost an ominous phrase, this, in his correspondence.[32] Finally, in 1537, he had to threaten them with the king's wrath and his own if they continued to infringe the privileges of the university.[33] The absence of further letters suggests that the town at last gave in, and with this surrender, after long resistance, to the power and patronage embodied in Thomas Cromwell the quarrels between town and gown were temporarily at an end.

3

INFORMING FOR PROFIT

An illegal story

That the making of a law and the enforcement of it are two different things is a commonplace which is nowhere more clearly exemplified than in the history of economic legislation. The point applied with especial force to the sixteenth century when the government attempted to control the economic life of the country, and particularly the export and import of goods, on a scale never before contemplated.[1] The problem was twofold. In the first place the administration of the customs lagged badly behind the rest of the financial administration. It was not until 1536 that nationally uniform rates were imposed,[2] and at no time could the central government be sure of effective control over the local officials, the customers and searchers and their deputies. While the royal lands were put under a modernized administration in the hands of such courts as those of General Surveyors and Augmentations, nothing was done either by Henry VII or by Thomas Cromwell to go to the root of the customs question. Cromwell admittedly produced a comprehensive code with a preamble which showed that at least he knew what the trouble was;[3] but, somewhat in contrast to his usual practice, he did not touch the administrative problem itself. The customs were left in the Exchequer from whose palsied hands the royal lands had been removed; consequently, when in an age of rising prices the value of the customs began to outpace that of fixed land rents, the government of Elizabeth could do no better than farm a revenue which its own machinery was incapable of handling efficiently. Until the reign of Charles II, the English customs administration was never thoroughly reformed, and governments fell back either on the inefficient Exchequer or on the dubious expedient of farming.[4]

But the unsatisfactory administration of the customs was only one part of a problem which also had its legal side in the whole question of the enforcement of penal legislation. If the state wished to prohibit some activity — as for instance the export of corn from the realm — it could proceed by issuing a statute or a proclamation which declared that activity illegal and imposed a specific penalty (usually a fine) to be levied on the offender. But before a conviction could be secured the case had to be brought to the notice of the courts, and, until the nineteenth century, the absence of a police force charged with this particular task made it necessary for the state to rely on the private citizen.[5] Of course, offences against the customs regulations should have been brought to book by customs officials, but (even if these had always been honest men) they were far to few and too busy to suffice by themselves. The sixteenth century therefore relied extensively on information laid in the king's courts by private persons, and in order to make such public-spirited action more attractive the law commonly offered the informer half the appointed fine for his pains. The other half went to the king, that is the state. The system had superficial advantages. It avoided the cumbersome details of criminal procedure with its presentment and trial by jury; it interested the largest possible number of people in the enforcement of the law; and it enabled the central courts to deal with offences of which they would never otherwise have heard. To its more obvious drawbacks – the delays of civil jurisdiction, the chances offered to chicanery and blackmail – must be added the fact that it turned what were really matters between crown and subject, matters affecting the welfare of the community, into purely private quarrels. This weakness was in no way remedied by the practice of associating the attorney-general in the prosecution of any case brought by an informer in which the king's interest was involved. The moral loss to the community was marked, more especially in such things as smuggling where opinion tended in any case to be against the enforcement of the regulations.

These, then, were the difficulties: the inefficiency of the customs service which made it impossible to carry out the government's economic policy, and the weaknesses of a system of law-enforcement which relied on informers. Both are well illustrated in the trials and tribulations of George Whelplay, haberdasher of London, who round about the years 1538–43 tried to make a career as an informer. It may be said at once that his persistence did not rest on repeated successes; he got remarkably little out of a bustling activity which, despite its essentially sordid air, had not a little of the pathetic about it.

It is possible that Whelplay had conceived the notion of becoming an enforcer of the law – or perhaps we should say, of making a living from breaches of the law – when, in 1535, he persuaded Thomas Cromwell to give him official backing.[6] On 4 September, Cromwell wrote to the mayors and officers of three south-coast ports (Southampton, Portsmouth and Poole) to inform them that the king

was sending down George Whelplay and John Brawne to
do 'certain business'. They were required not to hinder and
even, should Whelplay run into trouble, to assist him, if
they wished to avoid the king's high displeasure. No doubt
Whelplay carried this letter with him as a safe-conduct:
Cromwell's clerk endorsed the office copy as 'my master's
letter for George Whelplay'. The informer seems to have
struck lucky fairly soon. On 18 October, the mayor of
Southampton wrote to the minister to complain of his
protégé's actions. Certain citizens of Southampton had
freighted a Breton ship for Bordeaux, but it was seized
in the Solent by Whelplay and his company who took all
the money on board as well as a sealed bag addressed to a
Breton merchant. The master of the ship had lodged his
protest over this piece of piracy, and Cromwell was asked
to interfere. He seems to have instructed Sir Richard
Lister, chief baron of the Exchequer, to investigate locally,
and Sir Richard's report (written in haste on 8 December)
shows that Whelplay had in fact caught some mariners
in the act of smuggling bullion out of the country. The gold
was all in French crowns of the sun and hidden in various
places about the ship – 'as in pots, among floats and
tallow, and part in the top of the mast, and part sewed
with leather upon the cables and ropes'. Although Lister
advised Whelplay and his companion John Kyleby to
hand the money to the mayor or the customer, they said
they had put it in safe-keeping till they knew Cromwell's
mind. Whelplay added that he had already informed the
secretary and mentioned the letter of protection which he
carried and which guarded him against interference from
either the town authorities or the customs officials. They
had left for London on the 7th, assuring Lister that they
would immediately report to Cromwell. On this point the
chief baron felt sufficiently doubtful to express a hope

that they had done so, the sum involved being so large; 'else it were good to send to London with speed for them'. Lister had heard that Whelplay had been accompanied by five men when he made his seizure, and that he had already publicly sold 'the billet' and all the goods found in the offending vessel; now he was about to organize support at court to obtain the forfeiture for himself. Lister's last words suggest that Cromwell was little pleased with Whelplay for his high-handed action: 'If I can hear that they stay in these parts, I will cause them to come to your mastership . . . now that I know your pleasure.' The outcome is unknown, but it looks as though Cromwell regretted that he had given *carte blanche* to a man who had immediately stirred up serious trouble. At any rate, as far as is known, the minister never again employed Whelplay's services; in all the informer's many appearances from the Easter Term of 1538 onwards there is no sign that he was officially inspired or supported.

Whelplay opened his attack in the court of the Exchequer, as was proper for such revenue cases. All his informations started in the same manner, though they might develop in one of several ways. The record begins by stating that on such and such a day George Whelplay appeared before the barons 'tam pro domino Rege quam pro seipso' (a concise statement of the dilemma created by introducing the principle of private action into offences against the state), and that there he showed that he had confiscated certain goods or merchandise in some part of England which were being illegally exported, or which had been put up for sale in a public market although not made according to statutory specifications. Whelplay then prayed the court's decision and for himself the moiety of the value forfeited. These actions were started under statutes which arranged for the confiscation of the offending property rather than the imposition of a fixed fine; the principle that the informer took half still applied. On the information being received the court would either express disbelief and take no action – the informer would be 'non-suited' – in which case the record breaks off here; or it would try to establish the truth. If it felt this to be desirable it would, by writ directed to the sheriff, order the appearance of the accused. Sometimes the man so summoned obeyed; more commonly he failed to oblige, and in some cases summons after summons was issued, apparently without any kind of surprise, the case dragging on for years. Whelplay, for instance, informed against John Everton, haberdasher of London, who had put up for sale at Northampton market on 26 March 1538 quantities of ribbons imported from abroad, contrary to the act of 19 Henry VII c. 21. The information was laid on 15 May 1538; Everton was then summoned eight times in succession, one day after another being given for his appearance, until the record breaks off after the entry referring to the quindene of Easter (11 April) 1540.[7] The Exchequer, at least, took no effective action against a man who calmly ignored it for two years.

However, there was a way of securing the attendance of a man charged: the sheriff could be ordered to attach him. This was done at times, and at other times the defendant obeyed the summons. If he did so, denied the charges, and then 'put himself upon the country' (*se posuit super patriam* – that is, asked to be tried by a jury), the court would order the sheriff to empanel a jury of eighteen men locally and send them to Westminster to testify to the matter. This local jury did not materialize in any one of the cases started by Whelplay, and it is patent that this stage of the action was purely formal.

Having got it over, the court would then order the case to be tried at the next assizes in the locality where the confiscation had taken place, dismissing it there by writ of *nisi prius*. Naturally, such a trial usually brought into play local interests and prejudices, and the informer commonly stood little chance of getting his way. Whelplay, for instance, accused a certain John White, clerk, of Woodhurst (Hunts.) of trading in wool and cloth contrary to the statute.[8] After the usual preliminaries of information in the Exchequer, process issùed, defendant's appearance, and the dismissal of the case by *nisi prius*, White stood his trial at Huntingdon assizes. Here Whelplay, who made much of his expenses and trouble in the pursuit of the matter, produced what he described as credible and honest witness, to which White could reply only with a plain and unsupported denial. Nevertheless, the jury found for him. Whelplay complained to Star Chamber, and the jury were summoned and interrogated.[9] They explained that they had become convinced of improper collusion between the plaintiff and his witnesses who owed money to the defendant. The rights of the matter cannot be known, but (as cases to be reviewed later will show) the weight of probability lies with Whelplay. A Norwich jury, who similarly acquitted Thomas Andrewes and William Elwyn of the illegal export of goods, also had in the end to make their defence before Star Chamber, and a pretty feeble defence it was.[10] Whelplay, they said, had produced a confession from Andrewes, taken before Thomas Walsh, a baron of the Exchequer; but the document was not sealed, and Walsh had since died.[11] Admittedly, both Walsh and Andrewes had appended their names, but Whelplay could bring no proof that the signatures were genuine. One of his witnesses – Geoffrey Myghte, deputy customer of Blakeney Haven – had in the end given evidence against the prosecution's case. It was also true that Elwyn alone had been tried because Andrewes had not appeared, but as for the charge that he had disobeyed a subpoena they had only Whelplay's word for that. Even this single document – the jury's answer in Star Chamber – carries a strong suggestion that they did their best to exploit technical weaknesses in Whelplay's case, or even to invent them, so as to be able to find in favour of the accused.

In fact, Whelplay was successful in the Exchequer only on the rare occasions when the man whose goods he had attached made no fight of it. On 4 May 1538 he charged seven Devon clothiers with exhibiting at Philip's Norton (Somerset), on the previous 27 April, twenty-two woollen kerseys which in length and breadth failed to fulfil the conditions laid down by the act of 27 Henry VIII c. 12. They had thereby forfeited 36s. 8d. which sum they promptly paid to Whelplay. The barons decided that that was quite all right, took half the sum for the king, and left Whelplay with 18s. 4d.[12] On 7 November 1539, Whelplay reported that he had seized on a board a ship (the *Mary* of Portsmouth) nineteen crowns of the sun, valued at 4s. 8d. the crown, which belonged to William Pyke, master of the vessel; he had done so because the ship was outward bound, so that the illegal export of coin was involved. He does not explain how he came to be on the ship so conveniently or why Pyke surrendered his property meekly rather than threw the intruder in the sea. On this occasion the Exchequer made proclamation, 'prout moris est', for anyone to appear who wished to deny the legality of the seizure; as no one did, the coins were declared forfeit to the crown. Whelplay was charged with £4. 8s. 8d., their total value, and it appears from the record that he paid it; there is no mention of a moiety, and his public spirit does not seem to have earned him anything on this transaction.[13]

Another time he was a little more successful. On 17 December 1539 he seized certain victuals which were being exported without licence from the Suffolk port of Lowestoft. Once again proclamation was made, with no result; the court then had the goods valued and awarded Whelplay £5. 5s. 8d., half the value assessed. Whelplay, who of course held the lot and was charged with paying the king's share into the Exchequer, did not do so until 1549.[14] Identical action was taken over a quantity of brass, lead, worsted goods and victuals confiscated at Lowestoft on 30 March 1540 for the same reason; this time the informer made £11. 11s. ½d.[15] On 18 December 1539, during this profitable visit to East Anglia, Whelplay acquired some malt belonging to Robert Collimare of Great Yarmouth and handed it to Thomas Woodhouse of Wrentham in Suffolk for safe-keeping. Woodhouse was ordered to appear, but Whelplay came instead to say that he had received the malt from Woodhouse, and to be awarded 46s. 8d. for his share.[16] On 12 January 1541 he seized at London some parchment lace from an alien merchant, for which, after the usual proclamation and valuation, he received £2. 10s.[17] But that was all. For three years and more he sought out offences all over the country and plagued the barons of the Exchequer with plaints, and for it all he had a profit of £22. 11s. 8½d. It cannot be called a paying business.

More frequently, in any case, the court either failed to press the matter home or refused from the start to take any notice of Whelplay's statements. He was not often so unlucky as with John Peppys of South Creek (Norfolk), an ancestor of Samuel Pepys, whom he charged with having exported on 17 September 1540 quantities of lead and malt without payment of duty; Peppys unfairly died late in 1541, just as the court was getting ready to send the case to the assizes.[18] Between March 1538 and July 1540, there are eight informations on record which petered out, either because the defendant ignored the summons or because the jury trial went against the informer.[19] The matters dealt with did not differ from those already mentioned, except the case of Peter Tussey of Weymouth in Dorset, deputy to the searcher at Poole, whom Whelplay charged with keeping a tavern contrary to the act of 20 Henry VI c. 5 which forbade all customs officers to own ships or engage in trade. As we shall see later, Tussey was something of a personal enemy of Whelplay's, which accounts for the chicanery; it is not surprising that he got out of the rather frivolous charge by throwing himself on the mercy of a local jury. The places of Whelplay's activities also varied as widely as those in his successful cases: London, Stamford (North-ants.), Weymouth (Dorset), Shoreham (Sussex).

So far Whelplay had apparently succeeded in having about half of his informations taken seriously, and this may have gone to his head. At any rate, on three successive days (21, 22, and 23 January 1541) he carried out a general assault by bringing no fewer than fifteen cases in which he accused one East Anglian merchant after another of the illegal and unlicensed export of various foodstuffs.[20] Of twelve of these cases the court took no notice at all; the record breaks off after reciting Whelplay's request for action and his moiety, and the blankness of the membranes, contrasting strongly with their usual crowded state, is an eloquent sight indeed. In the other three cases, trials at the assizes were ordered, and in two of them it was returned that the accused had been acquitted. In the last, no return was received in the

Exchequer, which amounts to the same thing. Whelplay's great effort ended in complete failure, and from these blank parchments one gathers a feeling that the court was growing heartily sick of him and his informations. He tried once more, in May 1541, falling back on his early stand-by, the statute of 19 Henry VII which prohibited the sale of imported ribbons; but once again the court refused to look at the case, and Whelplay had to admit defeat.[21] All his vigorous activity in searching out those who broke the laws concerning exports and imports, customs duties and the proper manufacture of cloth, had brought him nothing but the contempt of the Exchequer. He had got very little for himself, but neither – let it be remembered – had the state been able to catch those who evaded its laws. It is on the face of it unlikely that all the cases in which Whelplay failed were unfairly trumped up, though those in which the court did nothing at all must have been extremely doubtful; the cases at which we shall look in more detail later support the view that on the whole Whelplay did not make up his stories. The fact was that conviction proved impossible, not that no offence had been committed. And one reason for this sorry state of affairs was undoubtedly that the Exchequer depended on information laid by interested parties and on the public spirit and honesty of local officials and juries who as likely as not were well in with the smugglers. That this is no fanciful supposition shall again be shown later.

Whelplay might be defeated in the Exchequer, but that did not mean the end of this remarkable haberdasher. There was one higher than the court of the Exchequer, and so he turned to the Council. His first reason for doing so would appear to have been the fact (not surprising in itself) that his practice of seizing contraband

and giving it to someone to keep safe did not always prevent the goods from slipping through his fingers. In October 1540,[22] he presented a memorandum to the Privy Council in which he alleged that Thomas Wood-house – on whom, as has been seen, he relied at other times – had let him down by buying up some confiscated foodstuffs which Whelplay had ordered to be kept till a decision was known. These goods, as well as others seized at Yarmouth, had since been shipped abroad. Moreover, some Flemings, engaged in the traffic, had got Whelplay into trouble with the lord treasurer, the duke of Norfolk, by complaining that he 'molested and damni-fied' them 'against equity and justice'. Norfolk had severely reprimanded the informer, but in the end had decided to investigate for himself. This brought Whelplay to the second point of his complaint, the countenance given by local customs officials to the local feeling which persistently prevented him from winning his cases at assize trials. At Walberswick in Suffolk, where he went to measure some confiscated grain for purposes of valuation, the customer at first seemed willing to obey a letter from the duke of Norfolk ordering him to assist; next day, however, he 'altered his mind', forbade Whelplay to go near the grain, and did the measuring himself – alone and without a witness. Unable to see justice done, Whelplay had turned for home, but not without collecting further evidence of the customs-service's feelings about him. At Snape in Suffolk, he ran across one Loder, deputy customer of the harbour of Woodbridge, who showered him with abuse, so as to provoke him to fury, 'whereby a fray might rise and thereupon a further inconvenience ensue'. Loder called him 'false knave, polling and promot-ing knave' – epithets which it is hard to deny had some relevance to Whelplay's doings, though perhaps they

came rather oddly from a government official.* The
informer, remembering the Council's previous goodness
in protecting him against such troubles, 'patiently suffered, and quietly departed, and kept his chamber'. The
document concluded with a list of 'the great conveyors of
corn' in the counties of Norfolk and Suffolk.

Whether in this paper or in yet another, the Council on
9 October 1540 received information from Whelplay
about 'untrue dealings' on the part of some officers in
various ports.[23] Such accusations could hardly be ignored,
though perhaps they were taken up the more readily on
this occasion because Norfolk, who as lord treasurer was
responsible for the customs-service, happened to be
absent from the board. On the 12th the Council informed
him of Whelplay's charges, mentioned that the king
desired the punishment of anyone guilty, and referred the
matter to his professional knowledge and long experience.
The move seems to have been turned into part of a
general administrative investigation; the Council added a
request for details of the offices and fees in Norfolk's gift
and made similar demands on other departments.[24] Four
days later – that is, by return of post – Norfolk replied
with an indignant denial.[25] If Whelplay could prove his
allegations, the duke would be only too pleased to see the
culprits severely punished; but he knew nothing of the
sort and did not believe that there was anything in it. As
was his habit, Norfolk took the accusation to himself and
defended himself against the unspoken – possibly even
unthought-of – charge that he had knowingly concealed
his subordinates' peculations and perhaps profited from
them. The letter is as peevish and self-righteous as the duke
himself, but little to the point. When, however, he turned
to Whelplay he hit the nail on the head. 'I do not marvel

* To promote meant to inform in the courts.

that Whelpeley has sought some occasion to get some favour; for of late his demeanour hath been such that – if it be true whereof I am informed (as it is likely to be) – I am sure none of us, of His Majesty's Council, would have attempted the like for right great sums.'* This is a justified reference to Whelplay's highhandedness in confiscating goods he suspected of being contraband; among the most amazing aspects of the story are the freedom with which this private citizen proceeded against mariners and merchants whom no one but he accused of wrongdoing, and the fact that they allowed him to do so without his suffering bodily harm. No doubt he made free with cries of 'in the king's name', as we know he did on occasion, but he certainly had neither official position nor official weapons to back such claims. It also looks as though Whelplay had not succeeded (as he thought he had) in convincing the duke that the complaints made against him were false.

However, even Norfolk seems to have thought that there might be some truth in the accusations; the very vigour with which he repudiated the charge of complicity makes one suspect that. Perhaps he had cause, for on 21 October the Privy Council were informed that a hoy laden with butter and cheese, arrested in Burnham Water (Essex), had been allowed to proceed on Norfolk's letters.²⁶ This was just the sort of thing to make any investigator suspicious. At any rate, the Council ordered the appearance of three Essex customs officials, but when they wished to hear the charges on 6 November, Whelplay and his assistant Ellis Brooke had to ask for more time to prepare their case. This seems to have annoyed

* The offenders of whom Norfolk spoke at the end of this letter were Yorkshire rebels who had taken refuge in Scotland; they had nothing to do with the business discussed in the first part of the letter.

the Council. They ordered one of the summoned searchers, whom they judged to be guilty, to be dealt with by Norfolk, but though they granted Whelplay his extra time they never seem to have taken the matter up again.[27] There is no evidence what happened, but that hoy released at Burnham hints at dark things. If in this particular case one may be guided by what is known of common sixteenth-century practices, one might say that Whelplay had been unlucky enough to pick on men whose influence with the Council was greater than his own. The Privy Council of Henry VIII's last years was particularly ill-fitted for the cleaning up of scandals. A single all-powerful minister like Wolsey or Cromwell might on occasion be bribable, but at least, if he wished to proceed against offenders, he could please himself. The councillors of 1540 had to allow for each other's corruption, balancing matters until action became impossible. Pushed on by specific orders from the king they might simulate zeal, but Henry's interest in administrative matters never lasted long, and things were presumably allowed to settle back into their old ways.

One other extant complaint from Whelplay to the Council may here be mentioned, though it cannot be dated and no result is known.[28] This was a declaration that 'by the means of silk wrought and brought into this realm contrary to the acts provided' the king lost heavily in customs duties and much unemployment was caused among native workers. Whelplay presented a good many facts of some interest, though one would really like a check which is not available. The increase in smuggled manufactured silk had resulted in a decline of the import of raw silk from more than 42,000 pounds to less than 6,000 pounds in thirty-five years, a loss of little short of £1,000 a year in customs dues and £10,000 in wages earned by silk-workers (who used to get, for throwing 2s. the pound, for dyeing 12d. the pound, and for weaving 2s. 8d. the pound – or 8s. or 9s. for special workmanship). A similar decline had affected the trade in 'short silk', that is 'the refuse of all other silk before rehearsed'; where 14,000 pounds a year had once been imported, barely 4,000 pounds now reached the king's beam (where imports were weighed for the customs).[29] All this 'mischief, decay and inconvenience' had come from 'the usage and acts of a small number of perverse persons ... having more respect and zeal to their own singular commodity than to the honour of their prince and common wealth of his realm'. As one who had suffered much from those malpractices, Whelplay had seized for the king's use 1,000 marks' worth of illegally imported silk goods and had entered his information in the Exchequer; he now prayed the king and Council for 'speedy suit and execution in and upon the premises'. There is nothing to show that they listened to this appeal or achieved anything for him on his other complaints. He had to content himself with having disturbed the dovecotes sufficiently for his name to stay in the memory; when Bishop Gardiner, five years later, wished to illustrate what would happen to the German Protestants who were troubling the world with their complaints, he recalled the instance of George Whelplay who had 'sometime' vexed the Exchequer with false information, only to see himself forced to come to terms and be non-suited.[30] At least the haberdasher had become a by-word.

Exchequer and Privy Council having proved broken reeds, there was still another chance for Whelplay. It was offered by the statute of 1539, 'that proclamations made by the king shall be obeyed'.[31] Though a special and very peculiar conciliar committee for the enforcement of proclamations was set up by the act, its chief effect was to stimulate recourse to the court of Star Chamber. In a few instances men laid information before the statutory committee; it was the body addressed by John Mascy, searcher for Chester, Liverpool and Beaumaris, and by Henry Sayer, another London haberdasher who dabbled a little in the informer's trade.[32] This is evidence that, contrary to what is usually held, the ostensible purpose of the Act of Proclamations was noted and exploited at the time, but there is nothing to show that this conciliar committee ever dealt with Mascy's and Sayer's bills. The indications are that the complaints were handled like all the others received by Star Chamber. Whelplay, in any case, addressed his bills to the king, as was proper in that court, though he too employed the act of 1539 as the basis of his actions. His opportunity came on 16 February 1541 when a proclamation appeared forbidding the export of grain and other victual without the king's licence, on the grounds that excessive exports were causing scarcity in England and driving up prices.[33]

Altogether there survive twenty bills entered by Whelplay in Star Chamber. They cover alleged offences against the proclamation between March 1541 and August 1543; eight belong to the year 1541, seven to 1542, and four to 1543.[34] One cannot be dated.[35] The places where Whelplay carried out his patriotic duty were situated in Norfolk (Lynn, Brancaster and Cley), Suffolk (Woodbridge and Ipswich), Essex (Little Wakering), Kent (Sandwich, Rochester and Milton near Gravesend – especially the last), Sussex (Chichester), Dorset (Portland – described in the bill as being in Somerset), and Somerset (Bridgwater and Uphill). To judge from the documents, Whelplay employed two different lawyers to draft his bills – there are two basic forms – but the burden is the

same throughout. Someone has tried to export quantities
of foodstuffs without licence and into parts beyond the sea,
sometimes in his own vessel and sometimes in a foreign
ship, Spanish or Flemish. Either there was no licence
at all, or the bond given specified a permitted port, Calais
or an English harbour; in any case, customs duties were
evaded, and the proclamation contravened, because the
goods were in fact destined for a forbidden port in Zee-
land, Flanders, France, or Scotland. Whelplay therefore
prayed for a subpoena to the offender to appear before the
Lords of the Council in the Star Chamber at Westminster
to answer to the charge. If his information proved correct
he would qualify for the informer's half-share in the fine
imposed by the Court, though of this there is nothing in the
bill.* It should also be noted that in these Star Chamber
cases, in contrast to his Exchequer cases, Whelplay only
reported offences and did not (except once) attempt to
confiscate contraband.

Few of the cases merit more than this bare description:
their outstanding interest lies in the number and geo-
graphical variety of Whelplay's ferretings. He must have
employed something like a small detective agency; it is
out of the question that he should have personally rushed
about the country in the necessary fashion, on the offchance
of getting evidence for a breach of the law. As a rule there
is nothing surprising about the charges: that a brewer
should smuggle beer, or a cornmerchant wheat, is only the

* The proclamation in question is not extant, but an earlier one of
November 1539, also concerned with the export and hoarding of grain,
specifically awarded the informer half the fine. It also authorized him to
sue in any of the king's courts at Westminster or before the Council as
appointed by the Act of Proclamations (cf. G. Schanz, *Englische Handels-
politik gegen Ende des Mittelalters*, 1881, ii. 669 ff.). This proclamation
lapsed on 1 Nov. 1540; it is probable that the proclamation of Feb. 1541
was designed to replace it and that it contained much the same provisions.

sort of thing one would expect to result from the prohibition. Indeed, the brewer (John Seth of Milton) explained that he had never sold beer except in the ordinary way of legitimate trade, though his defence was not strengthened by an unconvincing and suspicious plea that the proclamation had not, to his knowledge, been 'put out' in Kent.[36] A little more out of the ordinary is the enterprising shoemaker of Woodbridge in Suffolk who loaded eight quarters of wheat 'in a crayer called the *William* of Woodbridge' under bond to convey them to London; instead of which he – allegedly – transhipped the wheat into a Spanish ship at 'Hall haven in Thames' (near Tilbury).[37] Or there were Richard Saunderson and John Manby of Lynn in Norfolk who apparently went in for smuggling in a big way; Whelplay accused them of large-scale exports of barley to Scotland on two specified and numerous unspecified occasions.[38] One of the men accused by Whelplay deserves mention: this was Robert Reneger of Southampton who has recently been rediscovered as the first English pirate to capture a Spanish treasure ship. He, too, seems to have believed in smuggling wholesale, for Whelplay asserted that he exported a total of 700 quarters of wheat on one day from three separate harbours (Chichester, Arundel and Southampton), using three ships of his own – the *Magdelene*, the *Trinity*, and the *Jesus* – as well as one belonging to another man.[39]

A little more detail can be got in only one case where the deposition of a witness called by Whelplay has survived. According to Whelplay's bill, William Hyll of Minehead in Somerset put 216 quarters of beans in a ship of his own, ostensibly in order to convey them to Wales. However, two days later he had the beans transferred to another of those convenient Spanish ships 'riding in a place called the north-side of Bryandon', and they went to

Spain as unlicensed and illegal exports. William Harper,
a husbandman of Cheddar and clearly one of Whelplay's
agents, deposed that he witnessed the transfer and tried
to put out in a boat to seize the cargo; Hyll then ordered
his men to keep Harper off and if necessary to drown him
with his boat's crew. Four other Spanish vessels were also
loading in the roadstead at the time, but Harper did not
know with what because Hyll also prevented him from
searching those ships.[40] Even in this case, which on the
basis of our one-sided information looks cut and dried
enough, we cannot say what the Star Chamber made of it;
in no other case is there any corroborative detail. But once
again one is inclined to feel that Whelplay's informations
bear the stamp of truth, though it is quite another matter
whether he ever succeeded in proving anything and
obtaining his reward.

Whelplay's last appearance in the record shows him
reduced to fouling his own nest: after all his searchings
and seizings round England's coasts, he ended up by
informing against his fellows among the London haberdashers and by getting into trouble with the Company's
officials. The story is complicated and, in view of the
scanty evidence, hard to reconstruct.[41] It appears that
some time in 1542 or 1543 Whelplay charged Gilbert
Parvys, haberdasher, with having sold hats above the
statutory price of 9s. 8d. a dozen (in fact, at 13s. the
dozen), and that he sued in the Exchequer for a moiety of
£72. The case was remitted for trial in the Guildhall.
Whelplay's chief witness was Robert Watman, another
haberdasher to whom Parvys had allegedly sold the hats
and caps in question. After he had given his evidence, the
jury (no doubt citizens and merchants themselves, and
apparently got at by Parvys's friend Henry Smith), desired
a day – that is, they asked for an adjournment. When this

extraordinary request was granted, some of their number came to the Haberdashers' Hall to have word with the wardens, Richard Crymes (or Grymes), William Wood, Henry Austen, and Richard Alen. They said they understood that the wardens had previously investigated the matter and would like the benefit of their experience. The wardens told them that they had examined Watman on 19 January 1543, after Parvys had informed them (according to the custom of the Company) that Watman owed him money and that 'suit and variance' was likely to arise. Watman maintained that at this examination his alleged debt to Parvys declined from £17 to 33s., and that a proper study of his books would have proved that even this was due to Parvys cheating him by selling above the fixed price. The wardens, on the other hand, seem to have taken Parvys's side, charging Watman with having allowed himself to be procured by Whelplay in his attack on Parvys and trying to make him admit that all the business of excessive prices was an invention. This he refused to do. However, at the resumed trial in the Guildhall, the wardens of the Company gave evidence at the solicitation of Henry Smith and three members of the jury. Whelplay and Watman both had to be elsewhere that day, and the wardens' testimony secured Parvys's acquittal. The rights and wrongs of the affair remain obscure: as late as February 1544, Star Chamber, appealed to by Whelplay, was still trying to sort them out. Yet even if one discounts Watman's testimony and accepts the wardens' view that he was trying to bilk a debt to Parvys by alleging an illegal sales-price, and even if one agrees that the jury showed sense in wishing to hear the opinions of men who had already investigated the matter, it is hard not to feel that their action in themselves approaching the wardens and securing evidence on Parvys's behalf was distinctly peculiar, not to say highly improper. The wardens' depositions leave a strong impression that both Whelplay and Watman were disliked in the Company. Even on his own ground, the informer had to contend with the hostility of men whose first duty it should have been to assist him in seeing the law enforced.

So much for the general story which, by throwing a little light into dark corners, reveals a generous evasion of the law and some very curious consequences of the practice of relying on informers. The tale can be filled out from the rather fuller records of three of Whelplay's cases which show up more clearly still the kind of thing that went on and the kind of hazard a man ran who hoped to turn informing on smugglers and dishonest traders into a profitable business.

The first of these three cases concerned Thomas Vincent, a clothier of Winchester. On 6 June 1538 Whelplay appeared in the Exchequer Court to lay information to the effect that on the preceding 4 May Vincent had exhibited for sale eighty-nine kerseys, valued at 24s. each, without having them sealed by the ulnager.[42] From the later bill in Star Chamber it appears that (according to Whelplay) the cloths did not fulfil the statutory conditions of length and breadth and that Whelplay followed his usual practice of seizing them in the king's name.[43] He now made the normal request for the court's decision and the award of half the value – £53. 8s., for once a sum worth fighting over. Things then took their ordinary course. Vincent was ordered to appear in the octave of Michaelmas (5 October) and obeyed by his attorney, Edmund Rotsey. He denied everything and put himself upon the country; the attorney-general concurred in asking for a jury trial; and the court ordered the sheriff of Hampshire to empanel a jury and send them up to Westminster. Day given after day given passed by, with Vincent (or his attorney) present every time, but no reply received from Hampshire. Finally the sheriff (Sir Andrew Windsor, keeper of the Great Wardrobe and a loyal crown official) returned the writ on 10 April 1540, together with the names of the jurors whose persons, however, continued to be absent. Eighteen months had now been wasted, and one may wonder what had become of the eighty-nine kerseys which Whelplay had confiscated. If, as is likely, he followed his usual practice, he must have put them in the custody of the man from whom he had seized them, charging him in the king's name to be ready to answer for them. If Vincent was left to look after them it is highly improbable that he should have burdened himself for so long with the unwanted custody of £106 worth of saleable cloth, and the delay so far imposed very likely amounted already to a full defeat for Whelplay.

However, the court, patient for so long, now decided that some other way must be tried: a writ under the Exchequer seal transferred the case to the Winchester assizes to be held on 21 July 1540. Once again the passive resistance of the locality came into play, with all the power of the state apparently looking on helpless and unmoved. The assize judges – Sir Richard Lister, chief baron of the Exchequer, and Sir Thomas Willoughby, commissioner of *oyer* and *terminer* – reported that the jury had again failed to appear, and the record notes report after report of this kind until apparently the trial was at last made possible in October 1542, though the judges failed to notify the Exchequer of the outcome. The memoranda roll simply ends its record in the middle of nothing; if the law is an ass, it was a very patient ass indeed in this astonishing case.[44]

Happily the result of the trial was such as to send

Whelplay post-haste to Star Chamber, so that we can learn something about the events of which the Exchequer was left in ignorance. In his bill, Whelplay recited the start of the whole business some four or five years earlier, mentioned his attempts in the Exchequer, and described the writ of *nisi prius* which had ordered an assize trial on the issue whether Vincent 'had made, draped, and put to sale the said 89 kerseys . . . not being of length and breadth according to the statute'. On the day of the trial he left his home in London and travelled to Winchester, and there in open court, before the justices of assize and the jury (whose names he lists) he produced sufficient proof and witnesses of Vincent's guilt. In a way, after all those delays, it ought to have been a proud moment for him, but perhaps it was all in the day's work for a professional informer. He could even offer evidence, in the form of an affidavit from the town clerk of Winchester, that Vincent had before this been amerced by the mayor in the City Hall for a similar offence. But, however dishonest Vincent might be, no local jury was going to throw the local man to this informing jackal from London, and the trial jury brazenly returned a verdict of not guilty. Whelplay, describing this as perjury, pointed out that thereby the king had lost his rights and an evil example been set. He asked the Lords of the Council to call the jury up and investigate the matter.

Any suspicion of a false jury verdict always made the Star Chamber prick up its ears: nothing was more calculated to undermine the proper enforcement of the law and maintenance of order. The second paper in the file contains the jurors' replies to the court's interrogatory. They admitted — which there was no point in denying — that the *nisi prius* had been tried before the chief baron, but affirmed that the acquittal was right and proper.

Whelplay had failed to prove his case, and incidentally there had been no town clerk's certificate to prove Vincent's bad character. He had shown them 'an uncertain bill written in a piece of paper grounded upon the statute of Winton; which bill purported the said Vincent to have made certain cloths against the statutes of Winton and not against the statutes concerning the untrue making of cloth'; allegedly he had failed to explain who had written this scrap of paper or how he had come by it. We may take it that 'the statutes of Winton' referred to were the city ordinances of Winchester, and not – *per impossibile* – Edward I's Statute of Winchester (1285) for the organization of the militia and the police duties of the hundred. In that case, the paper so contemptuously described was presumably the document which Whelplay called the town clerk's certificate, and the jury were wilfully pretending that the only formal charge brought against Vincent consisted in an unauthenticated information alleging an infringement of a different law altogether from that for breach of which Vincent was being tried. Supposing this to be true, Vincent would indeed have had no case to answer, but common sense suggests that Whelplay is unlikely to have fallen down so completely on his job. Clearly, the jury, seeking an excuse for acquitting Vincent, found one of exceeding thinness which yet satisfied them. In his replication, Whelplay confined himself to a formal re-assertion of his accusation, and that is all the extant evidence. What the court thought of these diametrically opposed statements – nearly all statements in Star Chamber were that – or what it made of the jury's disingenuous evasion, we once again do not know. We may take it that Whelplay, at any rate, got nothing from it all, perhaps not even the satisfaction of seeing the jury, whose improper conduct had deprived him of £53, punished for a perjury which it is hard to doubt they had committed. Five years of hard work and long waiting in the king's interest but also his own – in his own interest but also the king's! – were plainly wasted, and incidentally Vincent had got away with a serious infringement of one of the most important of the government's attempts to regulate the clothing industry.

The second of our cases is rather more complicated. Once again it started in the Exchequer, so that there is a record on the memoranda roll,[45] though most of the details are to be got from the bill with answers in Star Chamber;[46] from these documents it is possible to put together a reasonably connected story. It all began on 5 August 1538,[47] when a group of nameless merchants prepared to ship from the port of Weymouth in Dorset, contrary to the act of 22 Henry VIII c. 14 and other legislation, sixty horses and quantities of leather, flock, wool, iron, salt, hides, beans, pewter, tin, lead, tallow and candles, without moreover paying any duty. The penalty for exporting horses was 40s. for each animal, and Whelplay assessed the value of the other goods at 100 marks;[48] thus a total of £186 was involved. Whelplay received information of the matter and immediately travelled down from London, according to his allegiance and bounden duty, and because he knew that much defrauding of the king's customs went on in those remote parts. Naturally, the thought of £93 lying there for the asking never entered his head. He succeeded in seizing the horses, and – knowing that there were three Norman ships offshore laden with prohibited exports – he decided to row out and make seizure of them too. There is no denying his enterprise, nor for that matter his courage. 'For the testimony thereof, as for his aid and succour,' he appealed in the king's name to John Raynold (deputy customer), John Clarke (deputy controller), Peter Tussey (deputy searcher),* and to William Randall and William Poynter, bailiffs of the town, to help him reach the ships; but they not only refused but used force to prevent him and saw to it that the ships put speedily out to sea. Tussey later told the Star Chamber that Whelplay ordered 'the passenger of Weymouth to set him with his passage boat' on board those ships, saying that he wished to seize their cargo in the king's name. Hearing this, the waterman (naturally) refused, whereupon Raynold and Clarke got Whelplay a boat; by then, however, it was too late and the ships had sailed.

These goods had escaped him, but at least he had the horses. However, he was not to enjoy them for long, either. When he went to inspect them in order to prepare his information for the Exchequer, the five men already mentioned, together with Richard Randall, a merchant of Weymouth, and others, set upon him, took the impounded horses from him 'vi & armis', and sold them overseas on 8 August, in contempt of the law. As he now had nothing to show he did not proceed, but a few weeks later – on 17 September – the identical chance offered. This time Whelplay says he seized 200 horses and that he made his appeal for assistance – undeterred, but also presumably because there was no one else – to the same men and Richard Harryst, the constable of Weymouth, and others. They not only refused 'in most spiteful manner', but ganging up on him with bills, swords and staves, they tried to throw him into the sea. In this they would have succeeded, he said, 'but for that he for safeguard of his life fastened upon one of the chiefest of the said evil sort which should have drowned with him.'

* All these men were customs officials at Weymouth, being deputies to the superior officers at Poole.

Such was Whelplay's version; the other side are also on record. It may be said at once that his story sounds the truer, though he certainly appears to have left out some parts which did not show him in a sufficiently peaceful light. Harryst, the constable, said that Whelplay, Ellis Brooke and John Dower, being armed, broke open a compound containing some thirty horses, which naturally caused a commotion. In pursuance of his duty, Harryst went down to the compound where he found Brooke with his dagger half drawn. He 'laid his hand upon the said dagger' and enjoined Brooke to keep the king's peace and surrender his weapon. Asked by what authority he interfered, he replied that he was the king's constable, to which Brooke's answer was: 'Whosoever shall take my weapon from me, he shall have the other end in his belly.' Harryst then called on the bystanders to assist in keeping the peace and disarming the strangers. He denied that there was any question of contraband.

Tussey, the man whom Whelplay later tried to get on a charge of keeping an inn despite his official position in the customs-service, deposed that there were then in Weymouth large numbers of horses ready to be 'conveyed over the sea'; it does not seem to have occurred to him that it was his duty to do anything about that. Whelplay went to two compounds and 'set upon the doors of the said pounds a mark of the broad arrow-head'; this must be a very early instance of this mark being used to denote government property. Tussey, with the others accused, was 'not content with the said Whelplay for so doing', so that 'words and contentation' ensued. He himself unfortunately and 'unadvisedly' chanced 'to smite and strike one Dower' who was then with Whelplay. The other allegations he denied, but he had admitted much – a good deal more than defendants in Star Chamber were in the habit of admitting. William Randall, on the other hand, would have none of the whole business, while Robert Randall thought he could get away with a very tall story. He, it seems, was the merchant behind the shipments of early August, but – said he – he then intended to visit Normandy to collect some debts and to trace 'a French lad' who had repaid Randall's hospitality by lifting some of his property before leaving. Randall asked the under-customer for licence to take with him one horse and one gelding. This being refused, he applied to Raynold's superior at Poole who ordered his deputy to accede to the request if Randall took an oath – to do what is not stated, but perhaps he was to swear to bring the animals back. As for the whole story of 17 September, none of it was true.

Of course, we cannot be certain what actually happened, but Tussey's frankness and Randall's curious tale together with his transparent effort to exculpate the local customs official go a long way towards confirming Whelplay's allegations. It seems likely that he did as he said on 5 August and was deprived of the fruits of his labour by a joint action on the part of the local population and the local customs officers. He therefore produced a show of arms at his second attempt but very nearly found ample cause to regret his boldness; perhaps his clinging to one of his assailants and threatening to drag him along into the sea really gave tempers time to cool just sufficiently to prevent murder being done. What stands out is the complicity of the guardians of the law in the smuggling that went on in this small and remote harbour; this also underlines how necessary informers like Whelplay were to the government. Undoubtedly Raynold and his associates could make much more by sharing in the illegal practices than by doing their duty and hoping for that famous moiety.

Anyhow, Whelplay put this information into the Exchequer on 26 October 1538, though oddly enough he confined it to the events of August. This time the court showed signs of energy. Perhaps the fact that local officers of the Exchequer were involved spurred it into action; perhaps it had not yet, at this early date, got tired of George Whelplay. The men accused were ordered to be attached, and all except Raynold (who appeared by attorney) were brought up on 29 January 1539, charged and committed to the Fleet. But the case was not destined to go so smoothly. The men put themselves upon the country, and the usual delays ensued while the court waited for the arrival of a jury from Dorset. Finally it dismissed the case to the Shaftesbury assizes where apparently it was heard, though the Exchequer was not informed and the record ends. In any case, before it came to trial, Whelplay appealed to Star Chamber. He had good reason to despair of a trial by jury at Shaftesbury where local feeling would as usual overcome justice. He told the Council the whole tale, described how issue was joined in the Exchequer, and added that he was offered a bribe of £20 to stay prosecution. This was later denied by William Randall who remarked that 'if he would have given a little reward unto the said complainant he should not have been troubled'. He may have been right at that, though Whelplay had more at stake than £20. The plaintiff went on to allege that the defendants had succeeded, 'privily' and 'through friendship', in obtaining a *nisi prius* dismissing the case to the assizes (this amounted to a charge that the court of the Exchequer was corrupt), and in having some of their familiar friends empanelled on the jury. Therefore, lest justice miscarry, the king be deceived and a perilous example set, he asked the Council to order the justice of assize to cease from intermeddling till the case had been heard before Star Chamber.

We know that the Court demanded answers to Whelplay's bill from the defendants, but there once again the evidence ends. It may be that Whelplay's case fared as well as it deserved – which by the extant information, is very well indeed. But it is much to be feared from the other cases known, as well as from Whelplay's later reputation in the memory of Bishop Gardiner, that he did not get very far in his fight with the merchants, mariners and customs officials of Weymouth.

The third and last case is least well documented. We have only a file of papers in Star Chamber, consisting of the answers made by a Suffolk jury to a lost bill of complaint from Whelplay, Whelplay's replication (which tells nothing), an interrogatory to be administered to some witnesses and the jurors, and a series of depositions to this interrogatory.[49] The case deserves notice because it throws real light on one of those jury trials on which Whelplay tended to come to grief, though in the absence of a bill or an Exchequer entry it is less easy to reconstruct the original accusation. The story apparently told by Whelplay runs something like this. At some date not recorded, Nicholas Smyth, (probably) of Southwold in Suffolk, exported to Rouen, without licence or payment of customs, fourteen fothers of lead and five great bells broken up. He first approached a certain Beamont who refused to have anything to do with the matter; thereupon Smyth hired John Purpet of Norwich to act as his agent for £6. 13s. 4d. Between them they broke the bells up 'in a moonshine night . . . with smiths' hammers or otherwise'; they then loaded a vessel chartered from William (or Robert?) Cawson with the lead and bell metal, covering it with 'eight chawlder of Newcastle coal'. Christopher

Usher was hired to pilot the ship, and the voyage was successfully carried out. The return cargo consisted of timber which was unloaded at Yarmouth and stored in a warehouse there which Smyth had rented.

Whelplay, having got wind of the transaction from a certain Richard Norton, laid his usual information in the Exchequer, and after the ordinary delays the case came up at the Lent assizes at Bury St Edmunds, probably in 1541 or 1542. The defence rested on the assertion that the goods did not belong to Smyth who had allegedly sold them to Purpet. Smyth's wife and father-in-law brought this tale to Norton in an attempt to get him to stop proceedings, but by then it was of course too late for that. Purpet was subpoenaed, but it seems that Smyth succeeded in preventing his appearance; also Smyth or his lawyers tried to get round the jury by suggesting to them in private that they had better decide the goods to have been Purpet's, 'for he was nought and Smyth had to lose, and where nothing is the king loseth his right'. Naturally all the jurors denied later that this interesting argument was ever put to them, but the story rings true and is borne out by the jury's behaviour at the trial. Smyth also attempted to buy off the plaintiffs by offering Norton £5, and to square Purpet by cancelling a debt of his. These points were confirmed by Norton and Purpet. In the Star Chamber Purpet was to admit that he had only been Smyth's agent and had never bought any of the lead or bell metal for himself. But at Bury, in his absence, the prosecution had to rely in part on the hiring of the warehouse at Yarmouth, for which they called a witness; this, they claimed with reason, showed Smyth to have been the owner of the return cargo and, to say the least, threw grave doubt on his story that the outward cargo had not been his. In part, there was the testimony of Christopher

Usher, the pilot, who, it would appear, properly blew the gaff. He testified to being hired by Smyth, to taking the ship (laden as charged) to Rouen, to the goods being Smyth's, to the hiding of the metal under the coal, and to the sale of it at Rouen as Smyth's property. But he had one drawback as a witness; he had a grievance against Smyth in the matter of his wages. According to one of the jurors, evidence was offered of a quarrel before the sailing; Purpet had then said, 'stick not for it, man, I will pay thee', and Smyth had added, 'go on thy business: he [meaning Purpet] shall pay thee'. The jury readily seized on this point, interpreted it to mean that Purpet was Usher's employer and therefore presumptive owner of the cargo, and – in the teeth of all the evidence – concluded that Whelplay had failed to prove Smyth's ownership. They therefore had no choice but to return a verdict of not guilty.

This seems to have been rather rather too much for the assize judge who, according to Whelplay, told the jury that they had not done well and warned them that he was referring the further examination to the Council. When questioned about this, most of the jury denied hearing any such words, a brazen behaviour which amounted to straightforward perjury. For that the judge had said something of the sort is proved by the admission of one juror who reported his lordship's remarks as follows: 'Masters, if ye be called by any person before the king's Council in this matter, ye will answer thereunto.' This may be a little less threatening than the version remembered by Whelplay, but it was bad enough and leaves no doubt what the judge thought of the verdict. What was more, Whelplay did not delay in bringing the matter to the notice of the Council in Star Chamber who extracted answers from the jurors and then interrogated not only them but also Purpet. The jury stuck to their guns, maintaining that Whelplay had proved the export but had not brought it home to Smyth; but Purpet, confronted by the might of the Council and the penalties for perjury, gave in and told the truth. He had been hired by Smyth, had never owned any of the smuggled metal, and had sold it at Rouen for his employer. This of course was the testimony which he would have given at Bury if Smyth had not prevented him from attending – if Whelplay is to be believed, and probably he is.

Once more we know nothing further about the case, but it does not seem likely that the court of Star Chamber would have let so flagrant a breach of duty and so plain a case of purjury go unpunished. The jurors were all little men – husbandmen, a tanner, a butcher, a yeoman – from whom nothing much in the way of fines could be collected; so, whatever may have happened to them, Whelplay presumably again was unrewarded. And Smyth, too, must have escaped punishment, for he had been acquitted at Bury and there is at least no evidence that the Star Chamber interested itself in him any further. Whelplay was deprived of his due, and the king's customs were successfully defrauded, because a jury of Suffolk country folk stubbornly rendered a false – a blatantly false – verdict. They were not intimidated: there is no question of embracery or even plain corruption, for had there been Whelplay would not have missed so useful a point. All that happened was that they did not wish to convict a local merchant who had done nothing worse than break those ridiculous regulations forbidding certain exports, and when a way out was suggested to them they took it with no regard for the evidence put before them. That was the sort of problem that Tudor governments had to solve in their attempts to regulate the economic life of the country and to augment the king's revenues from licences for export. This kind of local resistance to the central government's doings is less familiar than the problem of the over-publicized 'over-mighty subject', but by this time, at any rate, Star Chamber was much more commonly engaged in breaking down twelve bad men and untrue than in combating magnates.

George Whelplay's dismal career as a professional reformer displays the consequences of Tudor penal legislation and lack of a police force; between them, they produced this outstanding example of informing run as a business. He clearly had quite a nice little organization. Some six of the men engaged in the business with him are known: John Brawne and John Kyleby who shared in those promising beginnings at Southampton, Ellis Brooke who seems to have been a kind of chief assistant, John Dower who stood by at Weymouth and drew a punch from Peter Tussey, William Harper who watched the Dorset creeks and narrowly escaped drowning at the hands of William Hyll, and Richard Norton who kept an eye open for infringements on the Suffolk coast. Spreading his net all round the shores of England from Norfolk to Somerset, Whelplay must have employed agents in many places. But for all that he did not prove very successful. Highhanded though he was in his confiscations, frequent and eager as were his informations, and though in the last resort he could fall back on Star Chamber, he rarely achieved his object unless the other side refused to show fight. In his way stood, on the one hand, the complicity of the local customs officials, a complicity which he unsuccessfully tried to show up in his complaints to the Privy Council; on the other hand, there were the stubborn local loyalties of assize juries who rated perjury very much lower in the scale of crime than the conviction of a local

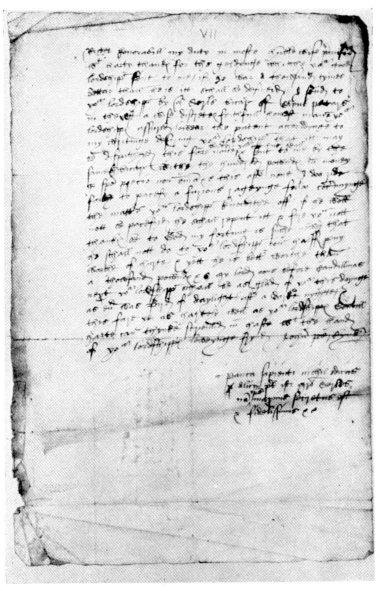

JOHN PARKINS TO THE ABBOT OF OSNEY

A PLAN OF CAMBRIDGE, c. 1550

SIR BRIAN TUKE, *c.* 1540

The Parish Church of St. Mary's, Hayes, Middx.

man on the word of a Londoner. These were evils, for the law – good or bad – ought not to be flouted, and it matters nothing whether one dislikes the busy figure of the informer or feels sorry for his pathetic failure. The same evils hampered the crown; the whole story is an eloquent commentary on the powers of Tudor governments. It is absurd to speak of despotism when the opposition of husbandmen and tradespeople could frustrate careful and cherished legislative plans, and when the great court of Star Chamber had to waste its time on the petty perjuries of local juries without in the end being able to ensure a proper observation of the regulations and the full enforcement of the law. But while this is true, let us also remember that we are dealing with smuggling. It took centuries to convince all the customs-service that they were really preventive and enforcement officers, and not men specially well placed by a kind Providence to share in the illegal traffic. As for the public attitude to cheating the customs, little has changed since Thomas Vincent, Robert Randall and Nicholas Smyth – guilty up to the ears – went confidently to be tried by their peers at the assizes of Winchester, Shaftesbury and Bury St Edmunds, and had their confidence rewarded by as improper acquittals as any on record.

4

THE TREASURER AND
THE GOLDSMITH

A cautionary story

The moral of this tale is either that one should never sign
a receipt until one has received the money, or that one
should not try to cheat a government department until
one knows how it works. Though, as is so often the
trouble with these stories, the full rights of the case and
the ultimate outcome cannot be established, one can here
get pretty close to them. The people involved are not
obscure. In the late autumn of 1537, Cornelius Hayes,
the king's goldsmith,* charged the clerks of the treasurer
of the Chamber with doing him out of £100. That
treasurer – Sir Brian Tuke, a civil servant whose career
began some twenty-eight years earlier when he became
clerk of the signet[1] – was still one of the chief financial
officers of the crown, even though the reforms of Thomas
Cromwell had already deprived him of the dominant
position in which Henry VII had established the office.[2]
Trouble in that quarter could be serious: if either the

---

*The first name suggests a foreign – probably Flemish – origin, a
conjecture supported by Hayes' own spelling of his surname as 'Haeys'
(*L.P.* xiii. II. 872).

treasurer was dishonest or his clerks had no difficulty in pulling the wool over his eyes, the financial organization of the state was in bad health. Hayes' accusations caused a rumpus in government circles, and a good deal of evidence survives from which one may reconstruct both his complaint and the accused men's defence, as well as something of the office routine of that distant bureaucracy.[3]

It appears that Hayes addressed his complaint to Thomas Cromwell, lord privy seal, who both in general (as the active head of the government) and in particular (as the titular master of the king's jewels) was the right man to approach. His story was this. On 20 July 1537, in the afternoon, he went to Tuke's house together with Gilbert Dethick, then Hammes pursuivant, to ask for money, saying 'it is time I should be paid'. Elsewhere it appears that the money in question was due on a warrant authorizing payment for the New Year's gifts which Hayes had made for the king, and one may feel that in pressing for payment seven months after the event he was, by sixteenth-century standards, unduly optimistic. However, Alan Hawte, Tuke's chief clerk, told him he should have £100 the next day. Hayes regretted that that day he would have to ride to the court, then at Easthampstead in Berkshire, to which Hawte returned: 'Ye shall not need to tarry for it, but set your hand to the warrant to have received so much and send your wife, or else your boy, tomorrow, or else when ye will, and they shall have £100 paid.' Thus quietly are great troubles born. Hayes was about to do as requested when Dethick 'rowned' in his ear: 'Will ye be so unwise to subscribe to have received £100 and receive no money?' Hawte asked what 'Master Hammes' wanted, and Hayes with a smile told of his companion's doubts. Hawte laughed: 'That makes no matter between us two: send tomorrow or when you will, and ye shall be paid.' Thus he signed the receipt, having yet had no money. On leaving, goldsmith and pursuivant went their different ways, Dethick to a shoe-maker's in St. Martin's parish. There he got into conversation with the man's wife, 'sitting in the shop'. He told her: 'I have been with Master Cornelius to Master Tuke's house where he hath done an unwise deed which I would never have done,' and all the rest of it; to which she replied that Hayes had 'played the unwise man'. The significance of this detail will emerge later. Hayes himself went to court and did nothing about sending for his money; on his return he and Dethick once again went to that shoemaker's place where the wife told Dethick to rebuke Hayes for his folly, but Hayes only said – one feels, with doubts arising in his own mind – 'I may have my money when I will, for it is sure enough.'

Some time later (he gives no date) he went once more to Hawte and asked 'if I should never be paid'. In view of his admitted omission to send for his £100 this seems a little unfair. Hawte asked his clerks to work out what was owing to Hayes and 'one named Thomas' – Thomas Knott, it appears elsewhere – said there was £300 unpaid on two warrants. Hawte promised him £100 of this next day. By Hayes' own account no mention was made on this occasion of the money already signed for but not yet received. There were present three men whom Hayes did not know, but 'having no mistrust' he omitted to get their names as witnesses. Early next morning, two of the treasurer's clerks, Thomas Knott and Thomas Carmarden, came to Hayes' house, 'and they bid me good morrow' – their ultimate villainy is underlined by this touch of hypocrisy – saying, 'we come to pay you money'. Nothing could be fairer, and Hayes replied jovially, 'he that bringeth money is ever welcome'. Thereupon they sat down at table and unmasked their batteries: they would pay him £6. 13s. in full payment for his warrant of New Year's gifts and another £50 on another warrant, for cramp-rings.* At this Hayes blew up. He snatched the second warrant from them and would take nothing on the first except all that was due; 'and calling them as they deserved to be called in so doing, I swore I would have the £100.' He went again to Tuke's house and met Thomas Knott whom he upbraided in the street, but Knott only replied that his master (Hawte) bade him 'do the worst and the best', he should never be paid. Twice thereafter he sent to Tuke himself, then lying sick at his country house in Havering atte Bower in Essex, from whom 'by his priest' he got only a request for patience till the matter were examined and cleared up. Tuke's clerks falsely persuaded the treasurer that Hayes had been paid the £100 for which he had signed, and there the matter rested.

The story hangs together well enough, especially if one can credit the almost incredible – that a goldsmith of all people should have signed a receipt for money he had not yet received. One of its weaknesses was the relative absence of witnesses; hence the stress on Gilbert Dethick's presence and the evidence, such as it was, of the shoemaker's wife who might be called to show that the story of the signed receipt was current before Hawte defaulted. When the case revived a few years later, for reasons which will appear in due course, Hayes had equipped himself with additional witnesses.⁴ He then put forward the word of another London goldsmith, John Chaundeler, who testified to going at Hayes' request for a drink to the

---

* Rings hallowed by the king on Good Friday were supposed to be a good cure for cramp and epilepsy; they therefore constituted a common royal gift and many were required.

house of a certain shoemaker named Peters, in St Martin's parish in London, on or about 26 July 1637;[5] it would therefore appear that Peters not only made shoes but also kept a wineshop, which explains those visits of Gilbert Dethick's in 1537. While drinking they talked of money, of which commodity Hayes owed some to Chaundeler. Hayes said: 'We shall have money, for I have signed a bill for £100 at Master Tuke's.' At this Peters' wife exclaimed: 'Jesu, Master Chaundeler, what manner of man is this! Chide him for that he will sign the bill and receive no money. An [if] I were the party now, he should have none.' 'Tut,' quoth Cornelius, 'my money is sure enough.' A few days later Hayes asked Chaundeler to come with him to see Tuke, on which occasion Tuke promised to 'see a way in this matter'. The witness thought that Hayes had been defrauded. Further support came from George Lambe, another goldsmith, who had been Hayes' apprentice in 1537. He deposed that he was sent to Tuke in Essex when Hayes could not get his money, that Tuke, being ill, would not see him, and that Tuke's chaplain had told him Hayes was to rest patient till the treasurer were well enough to investigate. These two, especially Chaundeler, added picturesque detail and little else. Lambe's testimony takes one no further, while Chaundeler's is very peculiar. It almost looks as though he was cast in 1543 for the part – or part of the part – filled by Gilbert Dethick in 1537; the fact that, as we shall see, Dethick rather let Hayes down may not be unconnected with this change in the story. In any case, Hayes' failure to produce Chaundeler on the earlier occasion, and Chaundeler's own interest in the money, render his word very uncertain. No doubt goldsmiths tended to stick together against king's treasurers who did not as a race treat them too well.

To return to 1537. When Cromwell received Hayes' complaint he took it seriously enough. Naturally he demanded to hear the other side, but while their reply was drafting he also addressed himself directly to Tuke. Hayes, after all, was a man whose word counted for something; he had been Wolsey's goldsmith and had entered the king's service as long ago as 1524.[6] It was improbable that a man so tried and trusted should make up so curious a story unless he could prove its truth. On the other hand, while Tuke himself was unquestionably above suspicion, he was a sick man whose repeated absences from London would give his clerks rather too much freedom of action.[7] If the office of the treasurer of the Chamber really lay open to this kind of malfeasance, the lord privy seal would have to see to it. Thus Tuke received from Cromwell what he described as 'earnest and pithy words' with a request 'to look substantially to this matter and to examine it groundly [thoroughly] without any manner of favour or partiality', and furthermore a detailed enquiry written, at Cromwell's instance, by Thomas Soulemont, the minister's private secretary.[8] His reply, of 23 December 1537, shows that the treasurer, like the honest and touchy civil servant he was, took the matter much to heart: he resented the implied criticism of himself and rushed to the defence of his staff. He was greatly worried by the possibility that Hayes' loud and repeated complaints might reach the king and draw upon the office the royal displeasure. He had therefore decided to stop Hayes' 'often clamour' by paying him £100 out of his own pocket, in exchange for a bond in which the goldsmith bound himself to return the money within eight days if Tuke's clerks should succeed in clearing themselves before Cromwell and such of the Council as he should call to assist him in the enquiry. Hayes promised to do so if Cromwell approved, as later he did.[9] 'This was yesterday and since I heard not of him.'

This was the reaction of a worried man who wished to prevent the spread of scandal; one might argue that his readiness to pay compromised his case. The second half of the letter displays him much less on the defensive. What had rankled most were some rather tactless phrases in Soulemont's letter, to the effect that 'like as Cornelius may be deceived so my clerks may deceive me, and that therefore in my proceeding in this matter I should take heed whether I were sure of their sincerity and truth'. Accused of obvious incompetence in office, Tuke was full of injured dignity:

> My lord, I say not nay but I am a man of so slender wit that I may be facilely deceived; but, my lord, not so soon by my clerks in these matters of importance as by others in smaller causes of my own. For by then your lordship shall have heard what orders I do use, which never treasurers of the Chamber did, between my clerks and me. Your lordship shall find that it is not very easy either for me or them to deceive the king's highness, or for them to deceive me.

This was a reference to the clerks' defence which contained a detailed account of the internal office organization of the treasurer of the Chamber. For the moment Tuke contented himself with assuring Cromwell of his absolute confidence in his clerks' ability to clear themselves and with asking him 'to persuade to your own self that somewhat is like to be said before your lordship in it otherwise than Cornelius hath said'. He would not write 'so largely' to one 'whose favour and good opinion of me I too much esteem', were he not sure. But annoyance and proper pride demanded the last word in a sentence in which Tuke justifiably complained that it was 'a hard precedent' for any treasurer to have to 'prove his payments against all such as would for their own lucre gladly surmise matter against it, otherwise than by the acquittance of the party'. There, of course, lay the administrative crux of the case: if a signed receipt was to be repudiated, what would become of the modern methods in finance with which both Henry VII and Cromwell had tried to leaven the ancient and cumbersome, but definitely safe, procedure of the Exchequer?

We may be sure that Cromwell was quite ready to hear the other side; the immediate doubts which both he and (more brutally) Soulemont seem to have expressed presumably took their rise in their close acquaintance with Hayes and in Tuke's frequent indispositions. Soon after this letter, the lord privy seal must have received the clerks' defence, a vast document which as now cut up and bound fills some twenty sides of large paper. A full study would have taxed the minister's time too severely, and he had two abstracts made (possibly by the clerks themselves)[10] – two, perhaps, because he did in fact ask some other councillor to assist him in unravelling the truth. The document was put in on behalf of Alan Hawte and Thomas Carmarden, clerks to Sir Brian Tuke, and Thomas Knott, clerk to Alan Hawte; internal evidence leaves little doubt that the treasurer himself took a hand in the drafting. Since, as they claimed, their answer could not be properly understood without reference to the charge it was meant to rebut, they first copied down Hayes' complaint, an act of kindness for which we must be properly grateful because the complaint has not survived elsewhere. Then they turned to their defence, giving a different account of events, stating the essential discrepancy between the two, and then (as they argued)

proving their case by reference to the standing orders of
the office. They concluded by adding several separate
points to strengthen the truth of their version.

According to Hawte, what happened about the disputed
warrant was this. Hayes' bill for New Year's gifts was
£766. 18s. 11d. of which by 14 May he had received
£660, a sum which included £100 paid to his wife. Thus
there was then due on this warrant £106. 18s. 11d. On
18 June he came to Tuke's house and asked Hawte for
some of this as well as some of the money due for cramp-
rings (£144. 11s. 1½d.). Hawte led the way to the 'scrip-
tory or counting-house, being near unto the gate,' to ask
Knott what they owed Hayes. The following exchange
then took place:

Knott: 'Upon the point of £300.'
Hawte: 'Be sure that I may tell my master the truth.'
Knott: 'Ye may surely say it is £200 and upward.'

So Hawte, in accordance with the custom of the office,
went to see Tuke 'in his gallery, where he useth to write
and do his business'. He told him that Hayes and other
creditors were come for money, and the treasurer, knowing 'that certain money was received and to be received
that day', ordered this cash to be divided amongst them
'as far as it would reach'. The hand-to-mouth existence so
typical of government departments in the sixteenth
century could hardly be more graphically illustrated.

Hawte offered to pay Hayes his £100 a little later 'when
this press is gone', but the goldsmith feared further delays
and politely insisted on immediate discharge. So they
went to the counter where Knott was at work on Hayes'
warrants. To him Hawte said: 'Knott, here is Master
Cornelius; my master hath appointed him £100. And
because there may be folks calling for money . . . I have

bidden him come soon towards evening and he shall have fair payment. And therefore, if I fortune to be out of the way, see he fail not of his payment.' Knott replied, 'it shall be done', and (turning to Hayes) continued, 'Master Cornelius, there is since ye were here last £200 delivered to your wife for the which we have yet no discharge. I pray you, sign the warrant for that now while ye be here.' After some hesitation Hayes complied. When Hawte returned in the evening he found the counter door shut because Knott and Carmarden were then busy inside with the books, and Hayes sitting on a bench by the door 'appointed for such a purpose'. Somewhat surprised to find him still unpaid, Hawte went into the office and told the clerks there: 'Sirs, ye be to blame ye dispatch not Master Cornelius; my master will not be contented if he knows that he be thus long delayed.' This constant use of Tuke as a bogeyman has a lifelike ring about it; its efficacy gives a rather more formidable impression of the treasurer than does his extant correspondence. Carmarden said, somewhat sulkily, that they had been very busy; Hayes would be the first to get money that evening. Finally they paid him, £90 in angels and £10 in English crowns.[11] When Knott wrote out the receipt on the warrant he accidentally put May for June, an error easily understood by anyone who has ever got the month wrong on a letter. But Carmarden spotted it: 'Lo, Knott, ye be so hasty and write so fast that ye do ye wot not what' – and Knott erased May and put in June. After reading it carefully, Hayes signed. By way of apology Knott remarked that though he had waited long the goldsmith had in the end had fair payment, and Hayes replied, 'So I have: I thank you for it.' He put the money in a canvas bag and the bag in a pouch by his side, and departed.

For some weeks thereafter, though Tuke remained in

London and the clerks often ran across Hayes, he never asked for more money. On 11 July, as Tuke was on horseback ready to ride into the country, Hawte reminded him of the creditors awaiting payment. The treasurer told him to come and see him next day or send Knott 'if there chance to be any business', and he would tell him what to do. On the 12th, Knott received instructions at Havering to pay Hayes £50 and tell him he would soon have all his due. On the 13th (and not, as he alleged on the 20th) Hayes came to enquire. Seeing there was but £6. 18s. 11d. outstanding for New Year's gifts, the clerks decided to clear this and use Tuke's £50 on the warrant for cramp-rings. So next day Carmarden and Knott, with £56. 18s. 11d., went to Hayes' house where till then they had 'always had good cheer'. When Hayes maintained that there was over £100 due on the first warrant he was told to add up the sum noted on it as paid and received, and on seeing a sum of £100 signed for in pale ink he burst out, 'By the mass, ye be false knaves; here is a parcel counterfeit that I have signed and is not in my hand.' The clerks replied 'if it were counterfeit, it were pity but were hanged', but Hayes repeated the charge. Thus 'they fell to multiplying of words'; Hayes snatched the warrant for cramp-rings and said he would not lose his £100 so; they parted in anger 'and no money there paid'

More than twenty days later John Halaly, a clerk of the Jewelhouse, happened to drop in at Tuke's office. He told the clerks that Hayes was spreading a story that they had forged his hand on a warrant and done him out of £100. To this Knott said: 'By my troth, I am glad ye speak of it, for ye know his hand and ye can judge whether it be counterfeit or not.' They showed him the warrant, and Halaly agreed that Hayes was lying: 'I will swear that this is his hand.' When Halaly so informed Hayes, the goldsmith, robbed of one line of attack, 'came to this new refuge' and produced the tale of the receipt signed without money being had, 'which thing he never invented nor spoke of before'.

So far the clerks' account. Its fullness and the production of a reliable witness to the story of the alleged forgery, of which Hayes had not said a word, at once tend to incline one to believe them. But they realized that their mere word was likely to avail them little before Cromwell and passed on to a very interesting and logical line of proof. They argued that the 'issue' – in the legal sense of the matter to be tried – consisted in the main in a date. Hayes said he had had no money from the Chamber between 14 May and 20 July; he denied having received any on 18 June. The clerks affirmed that he was paid £100 on 18 June and that nothing at all happened on 20 July; according to them, there had been no dealings with Hayes since the quarrel on 14 July. 'So as in the trial of this day will rest a great part of the trial of the whole matter.' Here they paused to register a protest – Tuke's protest, really – at having to do more than rely on a signed receipt; but since they know their account to be true they are content to prove it in detail. However, in order to do so they must explain the office routine of Tuke's department.

I have pointed out elsewhere that during Tuke's tenure of the treasurership of the Chamber the office acquired greater bureaucratic organization, and that this in itself was a factor in its decline because easy flexibility had been its chief advantage.[12] To start with, the treasurer of the Chamber had had the simplest of office organizations. He kept a straightforward record of receipts and payments which was audited by the king himself or (Henry VIII lapsing from his father's practice) by officers

specially appointed for the purpose, and later by the
general surveyors of crown lands; he paid on word of
mouth orders or on simple warrants signed by the king
and sealed with the signet; and in order to protect himself
he required the payee's signature on the warrant by way
of receipt (though this last may already have been a sign
of complication). This simplicity differed enormously
from the subtleties of the course of the Exchequer, where
every official had his double, nearly every record was kept
twice over by separate officers, and a profusion of tallies
and bills and entries built up a general system of defence
against fraud, though it also created heavy delays and
thorough inefficiency. Now while earlier treasurers of the
Chamber seem to have been ready to rely on their clerks'
loyalty and their own penetration to prevent peculation in
the office, Tuke – a good bureaucrat at heart – thought
it necessary to complicate the procedure at the risk of
slowing it down. As he put it: wishing to do his duty and
to have everything in perfect order both during his life
and when death had removed him from office, he had
taken such steps that he could not possibly cheat the king
'of a groat' without all his clerks – 'in whose danger he is
not minded to put his poor state' – being cognisant of it,
nor could they be untrue without his knowledge. In his
defence it must be said that he was throughout those years
far from well; also, he held in addition the clerkship of the
Parliament, an office which looked like a sinecure when he
took it in 1528 but had since, with the meeting of the
Reformation Parliament, become only too laborious.
Nevertheless, the real reason for his rules and regulations
was a natural fussiness and his fear of involving himself
in personal difficulties, a fear which we can perhaps understand better if we remember that Tudor treasurers stood
committed to the solvency of their office with their private

fortunes. As Tuke once told Cromwell, 'I must endanger myself for my furniture' – that is, use his own money for the official payments charged to him when no official money came in.[13] And so he did his best to make fraud impossible. If Hayes was lying – a point we have not yet settled – he was unfortunate in presumably being unaware of the new procedure which condemned his ruse to discovery; and Tuke could pride himself on having provided well.

The rules in question were two. The first concerned the books which had multiplied in number. The clerks in Tuke's office kept two yearly accounts – one for receipts and one for payments – which were called 'blotting books'; these, together with a record kept by the clerk who attended regularly at court,* were used in drawing up the balance sheet or 'original books' for the annual audit. But in addition the clerks kept another record called the 'book of natures' in which the particular coins of each payment and receipt, with the name of the recipient or payer-in and the date, were entered. These entries were always made at the time of the transaction and in the presence of the party concerned. Entries could not therefore be inserted out of their place or 'be afterwards falsified without open appearance'. The Defence transcribes the relevant entry of 18 June 1537, showing payment of £100 (£90 in angels and £10 in crowns) on a warrant of 6 February 1537 for £766. 18s. 11d., of which sum £660 had already been paid at various earlier dates.[14] The second relevant rule in the office compelled the clerks

---

* This is the only evidence known to me of a clerk being so employed by the treasurer of the Chamber. In view of the fact that the court was peripatetic while the treasurer by this time did his business in a regular office in London, some such arrangement was clearly necessary; what surprises is the absence of other references.

every day, after business hours, to bring Tuke a 'bill of the reckoning of receipts and payments of that day' together with the cash in hand (if any) 'sealed in a bag . . . and on the bag a label mentioning not only the whole content of the bag but also the natures of all kinds of monies in the same.' * Tuke entered the details in his own monthly book of receipts and payments and filed the clerks' certificate. The money was stored in an iron chest, 'standing in the surest place of his house' and provided with two locks; Tuke had one key and his chief clerk the other. To avoid all possible mischance, no one man — not even the treasurer himself — ever had possession of both keys at any time. If there was more money in the chest than Tuke thought 'meet to remain in his house', he had it conveyed to the royal treasury in the Tower where it remained at his disposal. If the day's receipts sufficed for the day's payments, the money in the iron chest was not touched; if not, the necessary money was taken out of it and immediately entered as paid. What matters here is the daily report rendered to Tuke at supper-time; this, too, was transcribed from the file, showing that on 18 June 1537 the Chamber received £255. 17s. 11d. and paid out £229. 2s. 5d., there remaining £26. 15s. 6d. for the iron chest. Those paying in were Bettes and Pawlshed, collectors of customs, Brewer, receiver for Bedford lands, Salamon, receiver for Warwick lands, Barton and Peter Freshewell, paying debts on bonds, and Mr Cely, unspecified. There received money that day Sir John Shelton, steward of the princesses' Household (£26. 12s. 4d.), Thomas Berthelet, the king's printer (£23. 4s. 2d.), Morgan Wolff, another of the king's goldsmiths (£75. 4s 11d.), Robert Grymhyll, a

* I.e. what coins the cash was in. This enabled the clerks to prove the payment in angels on 18 June.

messenger (£4), and our old friend Cornelius Hayes his disputed £100. Or rather, Hayes was paid before Grymhyll: the order proved significant.

In these details of procedure, important enough in themselves to anyone interested in sixteenth-century administration, the clerks professed to find the proof of their honesty. The 'book of natures' noted the payment to Hayes of £100 on 18 June in an entry so surrounded by others that the suspicion of later insertion must be ruled out. Moreover, Hayes, by his own account, never took exception to this alleged payment until over a month afterwards, by which time it was much too late for the clerks to doctor the accounts. The same argument applied to the daily return: they could not have squared this by some fraudulent entry for 18 June if – as Hayes alleged – they cheated him out of his money on 20 July. In fact, his whole story collapses because the clerks could not have asked him to sign for £100 on 20 July when, by their own records, there was only some £6 left unpaid on the warrant for New Year's gifts. Assuming the book and the file to be foolproof – and it is hard to see any weakness in their argument – the record shows Hayes to be in the wrong.

There is, however, one weakness, and the clerks both saw it and argued it away. They admitted that 'an ingenious or good-witted man' might allege that these proofs by the book of natures and the report to Tuke were nothing; they 'may be a mere fallacy of the said clerks prepensed and contrived before, for a preparative to deceive the said Cornelius when time should come'. What was to prevent the clerks from entering in both records £100 as paid and from later playing the trick alleged by Hayes on a man who trusted their good faith? A good deal, the clerks replied, in a tone of some satisfaction at being able to rebut even such 'ingenious' suspicions. If they had been so clever as to prepare this fraud, they could not have helped being shown up soon after as 'stark noddy fools and false harlots'. How were they to be sure that Hayes, unpaid since 14 May, would not come the very next day and all be discovered? The record once made was irrecoverable and they would have 'given it the adventure, hap what hap would'. In fact, they could never have taken the risk of discovery unless it were thought that 'they might do what they would, Sir Brian Tuke looketh not to it'. Against any such notion the clerks – or Tuke? – protest indignantly. The treasurer was the active head of the office. Not a penny was paid but by his orders, and none received unless he signed the acquittance or, if it was a question of a debt, returned the bond, all of which he kept personally. With his own hand he kept six separate account books – admittedly an irrelevant point but it 'should seem to be written to his laud'. In any case, if there was a plot, the clerks would have had to be sure of getting Hayes to sign a receipt for money not yet received, a likely contingency to wait for. He had never done so before: how could they trust to persuade him to it on this occasion? Indignation gave way to irony: the whole accusation, they say, bestows upon them marvellous powers of clairvoyance. 'God gave them some knowledge afore that Cornelius would not come for money of a month after or more, which was the 20th day of July, and also that the day following the same 20th day he must go to Easthampstead,' and so forth. The theory of a deep-laid plot will not hold up, and in that case the record must be allowed to speak convincingly.

There follows a short paragraph pointing out that further proof rests in the signature on the warrant, though of course this signature is what Hayes had been calling in doubt, first alleging forgery and then telling

his story of the signed receipt. Here the clerks step back
and the treasurer speaks clearly in tones of annoyance
which can be matched elsewhere in his correspondence.[15]
Both the treasurer of the Chamber and the cofferer of the
Household had always proved their payments simply by
the entries in their books, and there had been no call for
signed receipts or acquittances. This was so from the days
of Sir John Heron, the first great treasurer of the Chamber
after Henry VII's reorganization: 'to his book always firm
credence was given'. It would be intolerable if signatures
were made compulsory, and witnesses demanded to prove
the signature and witnesses to the fact of payment. No
such complaint as Hayes' had ever been raised; there was
every presumption against its truth; all arguments led to
the same conclusion; and lastly, the complainant was notoriously 'defamed in many things', though this was not the
place to follow up this charge. Surely, the case was clear?

If one can extract oneself from this weight of argument
and look at it without prejudice, it still looks good. If the
clerks had left their defence here – resting it on the discrepancy in the date and the full proof afforded by their
records – one would feel quite sure that they were speaking the truth. However, they continued their mammoth
paper further, and as one reads on the simple lines begin
again to blur. In the first place the clerks still had to
cope with that unfortunate erasure in the warrant. Since
the book of natures and the return also spoke of 18 June,
it mattered little in their view that 'June' in the warrant
was written over something else. Hayes, of course, claimed
that the something was July and that the erasure was
intended to square the date of his signing with the fraudu-
lently prepared documents. In that case, the clerks asked
triumphantly and reasonably, why was the date (18) not
also written over an erased 20? They admit that they can

hardly prove the truth of their explanation – that Knott had written May by mistake – but maintain that one can still read May under June when the warrant is held up to the light. They got in a hit at the unfortunate junior clerk by regretting that he did not have the sense to cross out and write over the line instead of erasing. It seems, however, that those traces of 'May' against the light must have been very doubtful indeed, for they dared not make much of them (infra-red light would have settled the matter); instead they had to fall back on their oath and the fact that it was the word of three of them against Hayes' single word. One of the three – Hawte, who had not attended the actual payment – was, they say, a disinterested party 'of as good fame, conscience and substance as Cornelius who is reputed in London for no perfect or rich man, though diverse of the court think otherwise'. This last remark must be remembered. They deserve as much credence as 'one needy indigent Cornelius in affirming a thing that neither hath appearance, conjecture, witness or likelihood'. However, the fact that laborious proof has now been replaced by simple assertion and personal abuse begins to undermine one's conviction of the clerks' justice and Hayes' villainy.

But we are far from done. The next proof, numbered the fourth – one, the book of natures; two, the daily return; three, the warrant – rests on a different basis altogether. When Cromwell asked Tuke to investigate the matter thoroughly, the treasurer, in fear of royal displeasure, called Hayes and the clerks before him and examined the latter in such wise that they came to think he was on the other side and not their 'good master'. That is what they say, and it is in character – in Tuke's character. From this document one can still get a feeling of the growing astonishment and resentment of these trained and

trusted officials when they began to realize that their
superior apparently believed them capable of a common
fraud. Their annoyance must have been the greater
because the examination took place in the presence of
John Williams (Cromwell's colleague as master of the
jewels), Thomas Soulemont (Cromwell's secretary), and
James Needham (clerk of the Works) who were presumably to see that Hayes got fair play and to hold a
watching brief for the lord privy seal. But the clerks stood
firm. Hayes had brought with him his one witness,
Dethick, but under Tuke's questioning the poor pursuivant faltered and admitted that he could not be sure of
the day and month on which the alleged signature had been
taken. This led Tuke to think 'his testimony of small
efficacy where the principal matter is forgotten'. He then
turned to and on Hayes, intending to catch him out.
Several times he asked him casually if he had had money
from the Chamber in June, the goldsmith agreeing he
had; and when the treasurer thought 'that the audience
might well imprint his saying in their minds', he
pounced: 'Master Cornelius, ye have confessed more than
eight times that ye received money in June, and my clerks
ask of you in all June none other parcel but this [of the
18th]; how say ye now to it?' Hayes was flustered beyond
hope of recovery. He stammered something about not
being all that sure of June – he had meant round about
then, perhaps 'at the latter end of May'. Tuke then showed
him that he himself had had no money in May after the
5th, nor his wife (if she was to enter the argument) after
the 14th, neither date 'at the latter end' of the month.
Then Soulemont interposed to ask Hayes if he could not
remember ever having had £100 in the kind of money
alleged, £90 in angels and the rest in English crowns.
Though the document is careful not to be explicit, a

suggestion is allowed to appear that Soulemont's intervention was intended to save Hayes from his floundering.
If so it failed: the goldsmith was apparently too far gone to
recognize a leading question when he saw one. He said,
yes, he had had such payment and would never deny it,
but that was two or three months earlier. In view of the
fact that the record proved such money to have passed only
on 18 June, the clerks argued that Hayes had virtually
confessed to have received the £100 in the manner maintained by them.

The agony is piled on: the clerks have witnesses.
Morgan Wolff, another well-known goldsmith, will
swear that he saw Hayes arriving at Tuke's office on 18
June, about five in the afternoon, as he himself was
leaving. There is no witness to the actual payment because
Tuke has ordered his clerks to keep the counter shut
when there is money on the board. But, as it happens, the
last man paid on that critical day, the messenger Robert
Grymhyll, impatient to have his money, pushed his way
into the closed office just as 'Cornelius was almost at a
point'. He will testify to seeing Hayes there with two
heaps of money, to hearing the exchange of polite remarks
in which Hayes acknowledged himself to be well satisfied
and to seeing Hayes sign the warrant – all on 18 June.
He can be sure of the date because he remembers it to
have been within a few days of Midsummer Day when he
intended to pay a debt of his own with the money got
from Tuke. This is confirmed by his creditor, a Mr
Gervayse. As against this, they say contemptuously,
Hayes relies on the testimony of Gilbert Dethick who has
married his maid and lives in his house. And Dethick was
so badly drilled that he could not swear to the date and
said during Tuke's interrogation that Hayes had told
him he had often had money without signing but never

the other way round – the very opposite of what Hayes no doubt meant him to say, for thus his word destroyed one of the pillars of Hayes' case. Admittedly, 'now that Hammes hath learned his lesson better' he will change his tale. In actual fact he accompanied Hayes in the morning of 18 June but stayed outside and saw and heard nothing; he was not present in the evening when Hayes got his money. The clerks thought that the story of the signature had grown up in this way: Dethick, somehow mixing things up, had come to believe that Hayes had signed without receiving money, and he had convinced Mrs Peters likewise. Thereupon Hayes, 'knowing that he had done no such folly, kept Hammes' simple belief and theirs in store and denied it not, thinking it might stand him in good stead that they took it so'. They thought this reasonable theory borne out by the fact that he fell back on the unlikely story after he had failed to bring home the charge of forgery.

Apart from a few summarizing remarks and an impassioned appeal for justice, this concludes the clerks' Defence. And a strong one it is, though it would have been even stronger but for the sudden appearance at the end of the inevitable eye-witness. If Grymhyll could really swear to that transaction on 18 June (and could really swear to the date), why was he not put in straightaway, without all the laborious parade of procedure, documentary proof and logical argument – or, if not without it, at least before it? I suspect Grymhyll of being a somewhat dubious witness on whom too much reliance could not be placed either because he could be proved prejudiced in the clerks' favour or because his testimony would not stand up to cross-examination. I should not be much surprised if the whole story of his pushing in and witnessing the end of the scene in the office were an invention, designed to balance Hayes' production of an eye-witness. At any rate I find that the theatrical *coup* with which he is made to clinch matters weakens rather than strengthens my belief in the clerks' defence. But before we can quite make up our minds on this matter we must look at Hayes' reply to this lengthy document.

This reply,[16] now partially mutilated, is an amateur's paper; as he says, 'I am not learned nor I am no lawyer to make so long process as they have'. It is full of appeals to the lords of the Council and fuller of bitter recriminations. Several passages in the clerks' Defence had manifestly touched him on the raw. They had accused him of 'a surmised and untrue allegation', as was common form in these written pleadings, but he took it personally and returned the compliment with heavy interest. They had deceived many others besides him, he had only once had money without signing (not many times, as they said), and so on. The clerks' rather contemptuous reference to the 'sewter's wife' (Mrs Peters) provoked this: 'I think, as I find, she has more truer honesty in her little finger than they have that call her so in all their untrue bodies.' The clerks had said, in an aside, that they had paid money to Hayes' wife and servant when the goldsmith was absent or drunk; disdaining to deny it, he answered that they would never be honest enough to get drunk, 'for it is one old saying that a child or a fool or a drunken man will ever show their conditions and the truth, but such as they be study ever falseness and dare neither eat nor drink and look if he hath hangen at the gallows one twelvemonth and more'. They said he was not reputed a wealthy man in London: 'I think it well, my lords, all for I cannot get goods as they do; therefore they think with their false-gotten goods and riches to overcome all honest poor men . . . I was a true honest man and got my living honestly and truly when they were not worth a groat.' It was small wonder they grew rich when they would 'beguile men so with hundreds at once'.

This is all good solid stuff – the honest craftsman in the toils of the subtle money-lenders and lawyers bellowing his just rage. It is, perhaps, a trifle overdone. In any case, it does little to the purpose, and it is not easy to disentangle answers on points of fact from this welter of injured innocence. In the course of his declamations Hayes seems to say (the mutilation of the paper obscuring his meaning) that the date could not have been 18 June because Hammes pursuivant was then still in France, whereas the clerks themselves admit that he was with Hayes at Tuke's house. This is a point we can check, and Hayes does not come out well: Gilbert Dethick had been sent to Stephen Gardiner and Sir Francis Bryan, ambassadors in France, but he had returned from there by 18 May.[17] As for the story of the transactions, Hayes repeats his earlier version very briefly and rather confusedly. He can bring a witness – John Hazelwood who was a teller of the Exchequer – to show that he received the £90-worth of angels long before Whitsunday (20 May): he used those same angels to pay a debt to Hazelwood. How very like Grymhyll's proof! The fact that even after erasure the date on the warrant appears as the 18th he explains by telling (belatedly) how the clerks were uncertain of the date, one saying it was the 19th and Hawte the 18th and that a day or two made no matter, so that Knott finally wrote the 18th though it was the 20th. It seems improbable that Hayes should not have made sure before he signed. Further, Hayes is certain that Morgan 'will not say he was with me when I subscribed that' – which is not what the clerks said Wolff would swear to.

Not all his tale was so feeble. He alleged that Grymhyll 'hath confessed it was long before Whitsonday that he did see me receive any money'. It is a pity we know no more of this, for it seems to confirm the doubts I have already expressed of this convenient witness. Perhaps Hayes was right and the clerks had overreached themselves in trying to make sure. He made an even more telling point when he revealed a new fact (or twisted a known fact?): if my accusation were false (says he), would Master Tuke have offered in his gallery to make a composition with me, which I refused, saying, 'I would take never a halfpenny less than my duty'? If Tuke had indeed suggested a compromise he was seriously undermining his clerks' case, but this is the first we have heard of it and the chances are that Hayes was misrepresenting the true offer of £100 conditional on repayment when the clerks had cleared themselves, an offer which has already been explained as due to Tuke's fear of a scandal and which Hayes, incidentally, either before or after this agreed to. Against the main part of the clerks' case – the proof derived from the office records – Hayes can say nothing. He falls back instead on the pose of the honest and simple man with whom these professionals can of course do as they please: 'Their books of long fables is nothing to me, for they have had time enough to write and to make what they list.' This is really not good enough: the essential value of the proof based on the records is that falsification after the event was quite out of the question. Nor does the goldsmith deal very successfully with the other most dangerous snag, the charge that he had talked of forgery before he talked of receipts signed without payment received and that he had never mentioned this earlier tale in his original complaint. He could only say that he knew there was more money owing to him than Carmarden and

Knott offered; he knew they had dealt falsely with him, and in his rage he failed to remember signing anything and – presumably – spoke of forgery before the matter became clear to him. That, at least, is how one may interpret his disjointed remarks on the subject. His reply ends with a request for a decision in his favour, so that he may be freed of his bond to Tuke: after all, he had his money and with it – as the sequel was to show – that possession which is proverbially so much more useful than any mere right.

At this point the documentary evidence ends for the first and most important part of the story. The clerks' defence carries a lot of conviction. There are weaknesses in it, notably that business of the witnesses at the end, but they can be understood as a somewhat unsuccessful gilding of the lily and look very small by comparison with the strong case built round the book of natures and the daily return. Also Hawte's lengthy and detailed account of events creates rather more confidence than does Hayes' shorter version. In addition, if Hayes did as he says he did he was a bigger fool than any king's goldsmith had a right to be. As far as we can tell it looks as though the goldsmith was trying to make £100 on the side, and if we look for a reason the number of debtors mentioned may suggest one. He paid £90 to Hazelwood; he owed Chaundeler enough to worry that worthy when no money came from Tuke. It may be that the clerks were right: Hayes affairs were in none too good a state. Perhaps the possibility of an honest mistake should not be ruled out, but I am not inclined to rate it very high. In any case, one may feel confident that Hayes had not been cheated of £100 and that there was nothing amiss with the office organization of the treasurer of the Chamber.

What happened next is rather obscure, but an outline

is given in that file of Star Chamber papers which belongs to the 1542–3 stage of the business.[18] From them it appears that Cromwell let the matter go before the Council. Hayes' bond to Tuke guaranteed repayment of the £100 paid to keep him quiet on condition – according to Hayes – that the clerks proved their innocence in full before Easter 1538, and according to Tuke on condition that the Council did not pronounce judgment against the clerks before that same date. This subtle difference was to matter, and it appears both from the event and from the fact that in 1542 Tuke offered to show the document in evidence that his version may be trusted. The clerks put in their defence, asking for judgment in their favour. However (says Tuke), no such judgment 'was then or hitherto given by reason that the plaintiff [Hayes] could not prove his allegation', so that 'the most part and almost all' of the Council thought him in the wrong. This is surely extraordinary: admittedly, Hayes was not on trial while the clerks were, but ordinarily, if the Council found against a plaintiff, it was quite capable of ordering him to desist and stating the truth plainly. Hayes only says that the clerks have not succeeded, or could ever succeed, in proving that they had paid him the money; in that case, if his account of the condition was correct (as almost certainly it was not), the bond would not have been forfeit. The conclusion to be drawn from all this is that the Council, probably under Cromwell's influence, saw well enough where the right of the matter lay but would not properly determine the issue. In effect they cleared the clerks but left Hayes with the money, incidentally accumulating sufficient material for further trouble.

If this attempt to penetrate the gloom has got anywhere near the truth, it would be interesting to know why the result of the enquiry was so inconclusive. One would have thought that Cromwell's view of the matter would appear either in Hayes' ceasing to be king's goldsmith or in a shake-up in Tuke's office. Not a bit of it; nobody anywhere was shaken up at all. Cornelius Hayes continued as king's goldsmith to his death, which occurred some time in 1546 or 1547;[19] as late as September 1545 he was accorded this title, and the last warrant traceable to him was ordered by the Privy Council on 1 July 1546.[20] Thomas Carmarden and Thomas Knott assisted Tuke's son in winding up his father's affairs after the treasurer's death in October 1545;[21] clearly they remained as clerks in the office. Alan Hawte was still Tuke's chief clerk in July 1541 when he replied to a Council enquiry that the treasurer could not provide more than a quarter of the £4,000 which the Council wanted him to pay for the expenses of Calais.[22] Thereafter his connection with the Chamber may have ceased – at least, the evidence for it ceases – but that was obviously not due to any repercussions of the 1537 scandal. Hawte appears repeatedly as a property owner in London,[23] until he seems to have died some time in the reign of Mary.[24] If he was no longer Tuke's clerk, the chances are that he left the treasurer's employ either to retire or to make a private living in London; after all, he had been Tuke's servant since at least 1528 and may have desired a change.[25] Perhaps he simply left the Chamber when his master died. The only effect of that noisy dust-up was one which in view of the language used and the recriminations scattered broadcast cannot surprise us: Hayes ceased to have any dealings with the treasurer of the Chamber, and payments to him were henceforth made by other officers, at first the treasurer of First Fruits and Tenths and later the treasurer of Augmentations.[26] Even this obvious change may at least have been influenced by the administrative developments of those years which involved the decline of the Chamber as a general pay-office.[27]

At any rate, it would appear that Cromwell contented himself with a typical Tudor compromise. Someone had behaved in a most reprehensible manner; and all the evidence pointed to the goldsmith. But Hayes had been associated with Wolsey, Cromwell and the king for over a dozen years, and – as the clerks had hinted so plainly in their Defence – he was *persona grata* at court. On the other hand, Cromwell had no particular liking for the treasurer of the Chamber with whom his relations were largely official: Tuke was a civil servant of the pre-Cromwell era whose career owed nothing to the lord privy seal, and his office was one which Cromwell intended to reduce in importance and scope. Nor, despite Tuke's conscientiousness and devotion to red tape, was it always as efficient and reliable as it ought to have been. The treasurer could hardly be blamed for the constant shortage of money, but his repeated representations and complaints are unlikely to have endeared him to the minister.[28] That his clerks took bribes is certain: not only did Hayes allege this in his reply, not only did Lady Lisle's London agent give them money to expedite his mistress's affairs,[29] but they would have been unnatural freaks in that age if they had not done so. No one, we may be sure, minded that, as long as the king was not defrauded. More serious was the sort of breakdown in efficiency which is exemplified in Tuke's books in 1540: when 'by Alan Hawte's negligence' an ambassador's diets had not been allowed him because the money had been paid not in cash but by assignment on foreign bankers.[30] Still, that is only a small point which should not detract from the general impression of bureaucratic order, combined with novel and much resented delays, which Tuke's administration has left behind.

Thus this storm of 1537 passed without a proper settlement. The goldsmith and the clerks, having fallen out resoundingly, were thereafter kept apart, but otherwise neither party suffered or won. Hayes could rest content with the £100 he had extracted from Tuke, though the treasurer still held a bond guaranteeing repayment. It is pretty plain that while Cromwell lived his protection and favour served to restrain Tuke from claiming his rights and to secure Hayes in the possession of his ill-gotten gains. Nothing further was heard until he had vanished from the scene. At last, some time in 1541, Sir Brian Tuke returned to the charge in an attempt to recover his £100. We know this because Hayes immediately rushed to Star Chamber with a bill which is the first of the documents in the file already mentioned. In it the goldsmith started once more from Adam. Once again we hear all about the signing of the receipt, the promises to pay wife or servant, the second visit and Hawte's allegation that he had paid the money – whereupon Carmarden, it now appears, interjected, 'nary mary, I paid it myself, for I remember well that thereof was £90 in angels and the residue in other money' – the whole helped out by the testimony of Dethick, now more impressive as Richmond herald, an office to which he had been promoted on 8 March 1541.[31] This provides an earliest date for this bill. The recital, which keeps clear of all the trickier parts, was only intended to set the stage for the Council in Star Chamber. Hayes went on to tell how the matter in controversy was put before Cromwell who, 'circumspectly pondering the same', ordered Tuke to pay Hayes £100 in return for that notorious bond. And now we come to the point: 'of late', Sir Brian Tuke, endeavouring to recover his money, sued out a writ of exigent against Hayes at the common law and had him proclaimed in the court of Hustings in the Guildhall, with intention to secure a sentence of outlawry. This was the proper though extreme procedure in a case of debt: the writ of exigent ordered the sheriff to proclaim a man in open court five times on pain of outlawry and to keep him in custody if he arrived. It was not usual to proceed to such lengths unless earlier attempts to gain redress had failed, for the writ was primarily intended for use against a debtor who could not be found; but Hayes alleged that Tuke had given him no previous warning. He therefore asked the Council to intervene and also to cancel his bond since the condition had never been fulfilled.

To this bill Tuke replied. He gave his version of the terms of the bond and briefly described what happened before the Council in 1538 – information which has already been used in this reconstruction. Oddly enough he agreed that he had paid that £100 at Cromwell's request – not, he insisted, by his order – though his own letter of December 1537 shows that the suggestion came from him.[32] He declared that since that crucial Easter 1538 he had several times asked Hayes for his money and that legal steps had been taken only when the goldsmith refused to honour his bond. There was nothing wrongful about the exigent or the proclamation in the Hustings court, and Hayes had now pleaded to it and issue was joined. In other words, the suit for debt of Tuke v. Hayes was dragging its slow course along in the Guildhall, even while Hayes was trying to short-circuit it by calling in the Council! The essential issue, of course, lay in the terms of the bond. If Hayes was bound to repay if no judgment was made against the clerks, then he was clearly in debt to Tuke. But if repayment became due only if the clerks were able to prove their case – that is, in effect to secure a judgment against Hayes – then Cromwell's tender regard for the goldsmith and the Council's readiness to leave the matter in suspense had given Hayes a way out. No doubt the bond itself would clear this up and may have done so in the Guildhall trial; unfortunately, we do not know what happened. I have searched in vain in the Record Office of the Corporation of London for any evidence concerning this suit of Tuke's or a trial resulting from it, though I have found a further sign of Hayes' shaky position in another suit for debt which had reached the stage of an order for distraint.[33]

Meanwhile the Council took some steps to investigate. The question of Tuke's suit for debt does not seem to have been pursued; instead the Council apparently intended to remedy its earlier neglect and proceeded to go over all the old ground again. But they either dropped it soon or the evidence has failed to survive: all we have are an interrogatory supplied by Hayes on which his witnesses against Carmarden and Knott (the only defendants now mentioned) were to be examined, and the testimony of John Chaundeler and George Lambe, taken on 8 February 1543, to which reference has already been made. If the Council got a little discouraged or thoroughly tired at this stage, who is to blame them? As always in these stories, what happened in the end is not known. All the chances are that Hayes got away with his fraud, for Tuke was dead within thirty months of those depositions being taken, and a sixteenth-century goldsmith who could not stave off the decision of a sixteenth-century court for that length of time would never have reached Hayes' position. Perhaps the moral of this tale should be neither of the two suggested at the beginning, but rather: always get a good lawyer and a better patron. It was the patronage and

old friendship of Thomas Cromwell which saved Cornelius Hayes from the consequences of a singularly brash
attempt at cheating a revenue office of the crown. Nor is
it untypical of Tudor administration at its best that the
only sufferer in the story was neither the government nor
the goldsmith, but only an honest if not very quick-witted
civil servant who may, for all we know, have been able
to spare £100 out of the profits he had gathered in a life-
time's service.

5

THE QUONDAM OF RIEVAULX

A cloistered story

This is the story of Edward Kirkby's deposition from the office of abbot of Rievaulx. It has been briefly told before, but the author of that article, published over forty years ago, was not aware of some important evidence and burdened his account with misleading preconceptions.[1] Perhaps it is not surprising that all monastic events in the decade 1530–40 should tend to be linked with greater events in Church and State: the Dissolution is commonly allowed to cast its distorting shadow both fore and aft. When a single London monastery is dissolved historians suspect a carefully staged dress rehearsal of the larger destruction;[2] similarly they ascribe the fate of Abbot Edward Kirkby to his 'opposing the king's new doctrines'.[3] But this concentration on the outstanding event is most perilous. The monasteries of the day do not seem to have been invariably aware of their coming doom; their history continued to be centred upon the narrower compass of their own interests.[4] We shall see that Kirkby's story does indeed reflect some issues of more general importance, but it is not true that he was deposed because he quarrelled with the new state of things or because the king wanted

147

him out. In fact, Henry VIII in person never enters
upon the stage and is likely to have remained practically
ignorant of Edward Kirkby. Like others of that time, the
abbot has been permitted to wear an undeserved, if
rather tiny, crown of lesser martyrdom – lesser because,
surviving the 1530s, he lacks the full qualifications for a
victim of Henry VIII.⁵ The facts must rob him of his
touch of spurious glory, but his unmasking may help
towards a better understanding of that troubled age.

The first inkling of something amiss at Rievaulx
appears in two letters from Rowland Lee to Thomas
Cromwell, written in May 1533.⁶ Lee, later (1534) to be
bishop of Coventry and Lichfield and Cromwell's right-
hand man in the marches of Wales, was at this time royal
chaplain and a master in chancery, offices which commonly involved a general dogsbodying in matters ecclesiastical on behalf of the government. Tradition alleges that
four months earlier he had officiated at the secret marriage
of Henry and Anne Boleyn, though there is no good
evidence of this. His presence in York and Bishop
Auckland (whence his two letters are dated) was due to a
special mission. He was engaged in persuading the northern province to follow the lead of Canterbury in accepting
the justice of Henry's divorce and its settlement in the
realm; in particular he had orders to secure the adherence
of Cuthbert Tunstall, bishop of Durham. A special
emissary was required because Wolsey's successor at
York, Edward Lee (not, as far as we know, related to
Rowland) notoriously disliked the king's anti-papal
proceedings. The north was already in that state of barely
suppressed excitement and resentment which in 1536 was
to burst forth in general risings – an amalgam of sepa-
ratism, feudal independence, economic grievances, and
religious apprehensions which Wolsey's indifference

had greatly augmented. The dispatch of a close associate of Cromwell's indicated that the new minister meant to keep an eye on this cauldron.

But great affairs did not monopolize Rowland Lee's attention. He took the opportunity to press upon Cromwell the concerns of the Cistercian monastery of Rievaulx, not far from York. He was writing on behalf of Thomas Manners, earl of Rutland, the founder's heir, who had – it appears – desired the king to institute an enquiry into the affairs of the abbey. Rutland wanted a royal letter authorizing Lee to investigate, but when Lee wrote, on the 7th, this had not arrived. On the 27th the earl himself wrote to Cromwell.[7] He gave thanks for the letter which Cromwell had in the meantime obtained, but this 'was not executed because that my cousin, Doctor Lee, had no time to tarry in the country'. He was therefore now so bold as to ask for another commission to the abbot of Fountains, Dr Marshall and Dr Palmer, 'jointly to examine and to order according to justice'. Cromwell was assured that by 'your favour herein ye bind me ever to do you such pleasure as shall lie in me'.

What caused Rutland to take this action? As founder's heir and patron he was certainly justified in interfering if trouble arose at the abbey, and his own particular person at once disposes of any suspicion that Kirkby was being persecuted because he was offering opposition to the king's policy. The initiative came from Rutland, and Rutland was no friend to anti-popery. As recently as February 1533 he had had a violent scene with the earl of Wiltshire, the king's new father-in-law, who had tried to sound him on his reactions to a settlement of the divorce issue in England, by action of Parliament. That is to say, he was being asked his views on the Act of Appeals introduced into the Commons in that month.

Rutland replied that the matter was spiritual and could not be decided in Parliament. Thereupon Wiltshire got abusive, and Rutland, as was the foolish and dangerous habit of the opposition peers, rushed to tell the whole story to the emperor's ambassador, Eustace Chapuys.[8] Later, admittedly, he came to terms with the new state of things, attending Anne Boleyn's official wedding as her carver,[9] but it is plain that since he led the attack on Kirkby there is no reason whatsoever to suppose that Kirkby was being subjected to a political persecution. The truth of the matter is that Rutland had received an appeal from a group among the monks of Rievaulx who later described themselves as 'we that are of your honourable lordship's party'.[10] As we shall see, of the twenty-three monks of the house, seven were hostile to the abbot and fourteen his friends, while two preserved an uneasy neutrality.

We have here, in fact, one of those distressing but not uncommon situations in later monastic history: an internecine split with violent accusations flying about from both sides. Kirkby, who had been elected as recently as 1530, had proved unable to establish his authority in a harmonious and decent manner. Some of his monks accused him of wasting the monastery's substance (a common enough charge in affairs of this sort),[11] while the chief allegations concerned his treatment of the house's dependants. Cromwell received documents intended to prove wrongs and injuries done by Kirkby to his tenants, as well as other information laid against him, though unfortunately all that survives of these are entries in his catalogue.[12] The main budget of indictment is highly suspect: contained in a letter of September 1533 from Thomas Legh who was then organizing Kirkby's deposition, it cannot be taken at its face value.[13] The abbot had

written a letter 'to the slander of the king's highness' and
imprisoned the monks who had obtained the royal commission against him. The slanderous letter does not survive
but in view of Kirkby's easy fate it may be supposed that
it did no more than protest against the commission. The
abbot had deprived one aged brother of the money with
which he was going to make his jubilee (celebrate his
fifty years in the order). All the country

> maketh exclamation of this abbot of Rievaulx, upon
> his abominable living and extortions by him commit-
> ted, also many wrongs to diverse miserable persons
> done, which evidently doth appear by bills corroborate
> to be true, with their oaths corporal in the presence of
> the commissioners and the said abbot taken.

All this does not amount to much, except to show that
there was serious trouble in the monastery of the kind
with which historians of monasticism are not unfamiliar.
No doubt the abbot had made enemies, perhaps (if that
aged man is any indication) by attempting to enforce the
discipline of his order. No doubt there was sufficient
discontent among tenants to exploit against him, for the
Cistercian houses of Yorkshire still retained their efficient
estate administration which must at times have been
galling. No doubt the abbot's enemies were no better than
he. As for accusations of dissolute living, these were so
much matter of form that the absence of any specific
charge may in itself be said to disprove them. But irre-
spective of the rights of the matter, it is clear that the
founder had to act when appealed to by a section of the
monks: something had to be done to restore harmony and
peace. Why Rutland should have taken the side of the
opposition monks we do not know, except that we can be
sure that national politics had nothing to do with it. In

view of Kirkby's short tenure, one may perhaps suspect some party strife at his election which his subsequent conduct failed to appease.

However, while some sort of outside interference in the affairs of Rievaulx had become necessary, the proper steps were far from clear. The Church had long possessed a weapon for investigating and settling troubles – the weapon of the visitation which combined enquiry, judgment and enforcement of decisions in one. The normal visitor was the bishop of the diocese, but most monastic institutions (except the Order of St Benedict – a large exception) had long been exempt from such local discipline. The Cistercian daughter-houses owed obedience to their founding-abbots and, above that, the whole order was subject to the general chapters held at Citeaux or Clairvaux in France, though Wolsey – ever anxious to increase his own control of ecclesiastical affairs – had committed them to the visitatorial supervision of the abbot of Waverley, the senior Cistercian abbey in England.[14] Wolsey could do this because his legatine commission made him pope in England, but with his fall the arrangement seems to have broken down and the order once again came under foreign control. The outcome was a royal commission of April 1532, appointing the abbots of Fountains, Woburn, Byland, St. Mary Graces (London) and Neath as visitors of all Cistercian houses in England.[15] The reason given was significant: it was thought inconvenient to admit the proper visitor, the abbot of Chailly, into the realm, since he, an inhabitant of France, was a stranger. So far so good; but it is hard to see what right the king had to interfere in the arrangements of the Cisterican order. Of course, the English Church had acknowledged him in January 1531 as their supreme head, a title which Henry then declared excluded all spiritual authority but which might well be held to involve authority to supervise discipline. It is also true that for many years the royal power had been invoked by patrons and others who found it difficult to get their way in specific cases, and that the king's virtual control over many abbatical elections justified some measure of interference in the conduct of monasteries. But all this as yet lacked the precision which the legislation of the Henrician Reformation was to give to it, and the story of Edward Kirkby certainly illustrated the difficulties yet to be overcome.

Rutland had thus taken the only steps open to him: he had asked the king to order the senior visitor of the order, the abbot of Fountains, to visit Rievaulx and investigate the complaints of the party opposed to Kirkby. The visitor's power, however, rested not on the rules of the order but on a royal commission, and by strict ecclesiastical standards the whole proceedings looked highly irregular. More peculiar still was the channel which Rutland chose to approach the king. Thomas Cromwell had by this time established himself as Henry's chief adviser, but he held as yet no office justifying his taking an interest in matters ecclesiastical. Nor was he to be principal secretary for another year: and the principal secretary was the proper person to approach if one wanted a favour from the king. Ordinarily Rutland would have turned to Stephen Gardiner, but Gardiner was in disgrace. The appeal to Cromwell shows how completely he had already concentrated all political power in his hands, though it may also be ascribed to Rutland's cousin Rowland Lee, a friend of Cromwell's. In the outcome it was to cause difficulties, and these in their turn led to results which almost persuade one that the most important aspect of Kirkby's case was its effect on Cromwell's mind.

In the first instance Cromwell, as has been seen, had responded swiftly, even though the commission to Lee, which he obtained from the king, proved valueless because the doctor could not spare the time to stay and investigate. It looks as though he was equally prompt in despatching the letter to the abbot of Fountains and the other commissioners for which the earl had then asked, but there the matter stuck. It was one thing to commission the abbot and quite another to make him do his duty – if indeed such an order from the crown could be said to embody his duty. Thus Rutland once again had recourse to Rowland Lee who some time in July renewed his representations to Cromwell.[16] He was careful to express gratitude for Cromwell's 'most gentle towardness and friendly help' in assisting Rutland's suit, though also smug enough to suppose that it was done 'the rather for my sake'. Now, however, the matter was 'protelated and delayed from time to time, without any good fruit coming thereof', and he hinted (though he would not affirm) that the abbot of Fountains was to blame. The earl and the doctor had therefore taken counsel together once again and decided – 'so it may so stand with your pleasure and not otherwise' – to have Lee's 'cousin doctor' attend when next the commissioners visited Rievaulx, promising this cousin his costs and 'also an honest reward to his contentation', that is a consultant's fee. Lee had therefore drawn up a letter of instruction to the commissioners which the cousin was to deliver to them as from Cromwell, and which no doubt authorized his supervisory part in the business. If Cromwell agreed to this, he would give Rutland so much delight 'that he shall have cause to thank you during his life for it: it is much to his honour, as the case standeth'. In this last phrase one may perhaps discern an explanation why the earl pressed so hard in the matter: it would appear

that his personal credit was involved in ridding Rievaulx
of Kirkby for the sake of those monks who had appealed
to him. Cromwell, on the other hand, was promised
nothing more substantial than thanks, a point worth
noting in view of current notions about his eagerness for
bribes; at the same time, in 1533 when he was barely
yet established in power, he would welcome the chance of
putting a peer – an opposition peer at that – under an
obligation.

Cromwell agreed to Lee's proposal, and by 16 August
1533 the cousin doctor had made his way to Rievaulx.
He turns out to have been Dr Thomas Legh (the spelling
being of course immaterial to the relationship) who was
later to acquire notoriety as one of the most unpleasant
of those whose general visitation of the monasteries
preceded the Dissolution. He was a young man, probably
about 33 years old at this time, and had taken his doctor
of civil law as recently as 1531;[17] in later years, as a
visitor and suppressor of monasteries, he was to have a
reputation for arrogance and insolence.[18] Perhaps he
displayed a similar temper as early as 1533, for the affairs
of Rievaulx did not get settled without some disputes.
Not that he began by antagonizing everybody: his first
letter from Rievaulx – 'where business is every day which
will be brought to effect according to my lord's [Rut-
land's] mind and yours' – was written to convey a request
from the abbots of Fountains and Byland, the Cistercian
visitors then at Rievaulx, who wanted assistance in dealing
with a monk of Holmcultram.[19] Actually, it was an
extraordinary request in the circumstances: they wished
Cromwell 'to decree a commission with authority unto
them, or license them by your letters, that they may sit
upon him [investigate him]'. When it suited them, abbots
and prelates were ready enough to accept the authority of

royal letters or even the letters of a mere privy councillor, a fact which explains much about the ease with which lay and governmental control was penetrating the defences of the Church. Rowland Lee soon after heard of Thomas's arrival at Rievaulx and wrote to thank Cromwell heartily 'for my lord of Rutland's suit'.[20]

For a fortnight Legh at Rievaulx wrestled with the reluctance of Robert Thirsk, the abbot of Fountains, who seems to have felt very unhappy about the whole affair, before, on 1 September 1533, he could report to Cromwell that his mission was accomplished.[21] His letter was angry and ominous. On arrival at Rievaulx he had presented Cromwell's letters of credence to the commissioners, 'which upon the abbot of Fountains' part was but lightly regarded'. Thirsk argued that 'such letters as I delivered and credence related was from Master Cromwell only and not from the king's highness'. He had a point: there was no reason whatsoever why he should permit a brash young lawyer to assert a right to control his actions merely because one of the king's councillors said so. However, he could not brush Legh off so easily. It seems that the proceedings then got under way. The charges against Kirkby were investigated and proved by witnesses; Legh alleged sixteen of them, as well as affidavits and even a confession on Kirkby's part. It is impossible to doubt that a case could be made against him; he had clearly behaved in a somewhat overbearing fashion, had asserted his abbatical authority unwisely both inside and outside the house, and had deserved censure, though Legh was probably exaggerating the hostile feelings of the countryside. But the abbot of Fountains had no intention of deposing his colleague. He took exception to his commission, claimed that it gave no authority either to him or to anyone else to proceed against the abbot of Rievaulx, and for good measure assembled a series of legal objections to the king's letters. They were deceitful and deceitfully obtained, being extracted from the king by a suppression of the truth and an affirmation of what was false, and he did not feel bound to obey them. To cap it all, 'in his obstinacy and perverse mind, adhering to the rules of his religion (as he said)', he departed from Rievaulx without waiting to carry out the king's command. All Legh's pressure – he even ordered him in the king's name 'to tarry and make process according to justice without further delay' – could not prevail. For an excuse he pleaded affairs of his own. He had heard that the earl of Cumberland had obtained a commission to enquire into some titles to land and felt he ought to be on his own estates to keep a watchful eye, 'nam tunc sua res agitur paries cum proximus ardet'. Legh, in disgust, held that all this only displayed 'his 'rebellious mind' of which 'many of that religion' were guilty. Kirkby had reacted to the enquiry by taking steps against his accusers among his own monks and had also written the letter, now lost, which Legh described as slanderous. It is probable that both Kirkby and Thirsk had expressed opposition to the royal interference in monastic matters, for Legh said that they

as persons almost nothing regarding God and very little our great master, the king, under the pretence of the rules of their religion liveth as persons *solute ab omni lege seu obediencia et Deo et regi debita*, being aboutwards, as it seemeth to me, to rule the king by their rules, which is a perverse order that so noble a head should be ruled by so putrid and most corrupt members.

The troubles at Rievaulx had not originally begun for political reasons, but the attempt to settle them underlined the inadequacy of the royal weapons of control and revealed the latent hostility to secular interference which was to call so many monks (Thirsk among them) into the ranks of the Pilgrims of Grace.

Though the abbot of Fountains would not stay to see the matter through, the other commissioners proved less scrupulous. As Legh put it, they 'proceeded according to the law and your credence by me to them related' by removing Kirkby from the rule and administration of the abbey. Thus Rutland had achieved his immediate ends. But since the chief visitor and only abbot among them had refused to act, the deposition was apparently carried out by two doctors of law, supervised by a third, not one of whom was a Cistercian or even a monk. Small wonder that Kirkby's party remained unconvinced. For Legh the affair carried a far-reaching lesson.

> Therefore, *tempore iam instante*, the king's majesty considered (whom they have acknowledged to be *supremum caput totius ecclesie Anglicane*), the honour of my lord of Rutland in this business remembered, your worship and also my poor honesty not forgotten, they would either quickly be looked upon and shortly, or else their dissolute living with rebellious demeanour shall every day increase more and more, to the displeasure of God, disquietude of the king's prerogative, and reproach of slanders unto their religion, with trouble of such countries as they are inhabited in.

He recurred to his point in a postcript:

> I pray you, note their presumptuous minds, most alien-ate from religion, having nothing of their own ne may have their accounts made, which – only to be called an abbot – will contend contrary to their obedience with

the king's highness, the founders and all other, to the
slander of the religion, disquietness and extreme costs
and charges of their house.

His experiences at Rievaulx convinced Legh that the
orders needed thoroughly investigating and reforming.
When two years later he travelled from monastery to
monastery, many men had cause to regret the contempt
with which the abbot of Fountains had treated him in
1533 – the hurt to his 'poor honesty' – and the impression
left by Edward Kirkby who seemed ready to ignore all
his duty and the respect due to authority in his eager
pursuit of the empty title and office of abbot. Of course,
this was a prejudiced and unfair view: Kirkby had been
canonically elected, and the senior visitor of his order
declared himself unqualified to depose him. Nevertheless,
Legh's feelings, so important for the future, are highly
significant as showing the temper of the younger clerical
careerists who were ready to serve secular authority; his
diagnosis that the conflict between the king's command
and the rules of the order must be resolved in favour
of the former was a shrewd appraisal of the situation.

In any case, at Rievaulx the king and Rutland between
them had outflanked the scruples of the abbot of Fountains, and Kirkby was out of his abbacy. But now a
successor had to be found. The election of an abbot was
in the hands of the monks themselves, though they
required the licence of their patron, a favour which in
this case the earl naturally granted readily. But it quickly
became apparent that of their own free will the monks of
Rievaulx would never proceed to an election: a majority
still thought Kirkby improperly deposed. Having interfered so far, the king – or rather Cromwell – could not
now draw back. Since government pressure had secured

Kirkby's removal, it was up to the government to obtain
the appointment of a successor and avoid the scandal and
inconvenience of a long vacancy. Thus, on 13 September
1533, a letter commissive under the royal signet and sign
manual ordered the abbots of Fountains and Byland to
smooth the way to an election at Rievaulx.[22] The letter
went over the earlier business. It recalled how, at the
humble suit of the earl of Rutland, the king had appointed
commissioners to enquire 'in due form' into the behaviour
of Abbot Edward and – 'if they found him of misorder
and [evil] living' – to depose him 'by order of the law and
virtue of our said commission'. They having done so, the
monastery now stood vacant, and the two abbots were
therefore ordered to repair to Rievaulx

> to procure by all lawful means and ways ye can the
> convent of the same to proceed with the licence of our
> said cousin their patron [Rutland] to the election of a
> new abbot, and to certify unto us all that ye and the
> said convent shall have done therein; for that we much
> desire the good establishment of the said monastery, as
> we do of all others.

They were told to see the matter speedily accomplished,
using all their diligence, learning, wisdom, and good
dexterity. It is only an impression, but to me some of
those phrases, which were far from common form, sound
like the language of Cromwell.

The abbot of Byland received the commission on 22
September. It was delivered to him 'by the hands of my
father, the abbot of Rievaulx', a term which at that time
he can only have applied to Kirkby. But Kirkby was already deposed and at best the late or 'quondam' abbot of
Rievaulx. It portented little hope of a speedy success to
his mission if the commissioner himself treated the deposi-

tion as invalid. If he really thought Kirkby still abbot, how could he be expected to obtain a new election to a place he apparently refused to consider vacant? Kirkby's part in the business is equally curious. It must be supposed that he had decided to make the best of a bad job and to win favour at court, not so much, perhaps, in hopes of having his deposition yet rescinded but with an eye to the pension which his successor would be obliged to pay him. It looks as though his offer to act as messenger for the commission ordering a new election was meant to display his willingness to submit and create a good impression. In this he seems to have succeeded: when he came to fight for his pension he did indeed have Cromwell on his side.

Taking his time, the abbot of Byland finally put in an appearance at Rievaulx on 15 October. He was alone because the abbot of Fountains had had to carry out another royal commission concerning the election of a new abbot at Combermere in Cheshire, a relief for which, one suspects, he secretly gave much thanks.[23] The lone commissioner at Rievaulx brought with him a public notary (Brian Lewty), his own prior (Robert Harom), and his chaplain (Thomas Wenseley), to witness his proceedings. These consisted of his calling before him each of the twenty-three monks of Rievaulx and examining them individually 'according to the statutes of my religion'.[24] Kirkby prudently absented himself. None of the men knew what the other brethren had said. The abbot maintained that he had 'exhorted, advertised and induced' them all to proceed to the election 'according to the tenor and effect of your grace's said commission'. In fact he did nothing so like his duty, for he confined himself to asking each monk this tendentious question: 'Think ye that your father abbot is lawfully deposed or will ye have your election of a new abbot according to the king's commission?'[25] The result was not encouraging. Of the twenty-three, no fewer than fourteen, led by the subprior, William Storrer, declared themselves unable to elect 'forasmuch as the said monastery is not vacant, because his father abbot Dan Edward Kirkby was not deposed, nor is, lawfully according to the rules and statutes of their religion'.* Though the monks did not know each other's answers, they had clearly, and naturally, concerted their replies beforehand; with small differences they all said the same thing. The deposition of Edward Kirkby had not been lawful, being contrary to the rules of their order, and the question of a new election did not therefore arise. Their position, amounting to a straightforward rejection of the king's commission, had, as far as we know, the tacit support of the abbots of Fountains and Byland and was quite sound in law, simply because the relation of the king's ecclesiastical authority to such administrative details as monastic visitations and discipline had not yet been clarified. Seven monks† announced themselves ready to make a new election, but their answers were less uniform. Only two specifically declared that Kirkby's deposition was 'secundum leges'; one wished to obey the founder's desires; the other four simply said they would elect. But in view of the line taken by the abbot of Byland they hardly had occasion to say more. This diversity of expression is a sign of insufficient

* The other thirteen were Stephen Burght, Robert Standrop, Robert Pykering, Thomas Yarom, Richard Alverton, Richard Rypon, Richard Gryllyng, Henry Thrysk, William Tanfeld, James Guysburn, Christopher Helmysley, Oliver Broughton, and William Darneton.

† William Yeresley, Richard Scarburgh, John Malton, Thomas Richmond, Roger Whytby, William Bedall, John Lyn. These, like the rest, are of course mostly place names – no doubt of the places whence these men came. Their proper surnames, abandoned on entering the order, are recorded in the pension list of 1539 (*L.P.* xiv. i. 185).

rehearsal rather than uncertainty among the party hostile
to Kirkby, which in any case was soon to show its soli-
darity.[26] Matthew Ampleforth sat on the fence: he denied
the deposition to be lawful but was ready 'to conform him
to the king's pleasure and the founder'. More delicately
still, William Farlyngton simply offered 'to be obedient
to the fathers of their religion, and as they proceed to an
election, so will he'. Certainly the king's commission
caused no transports of joy at Rievaulx.

The abbot of Byland simply recorded these points of
view and certified the king and Council of their existence,
but even though he added that he was acting 'most
humbly, lowly and meekly' he could not disguise the
fact that he had executed his commission very insuffi-
ciently. Instructed to use 'all lawful means and ways' to
get a new abbot elected, he had contented himself with
collecting and presenting evidence that the majority of
the electors thought themselves unable to act. In a
narrow way he had observed the letter of his orders, but
at the very least he was guilty of skilful passive resistance.
This was not what the government had meant him to do,
as he must have known perfectly well; and he was mistaken if he thought he could get away with it. The other
side would not let things rest in his carefully contrived
cul-de-sac. On the day after his futile proceedings (16
October) the seven monks of Rutland's party wrote a
hurried and anxious letter to the founder.[27] They had
naturally imagined that the abbot's arrival would herald
an election, instead of which he had sat 'after the fashion
of an enquiry in a chamber secret and not in our chapter-
house according to the custom of our religion'. They
complained of the individual interrogation and of the form
of the question put to them. The other party, they alleged,
received encouragement from Kirkby and even from the

commissioner himself. Kirkby continued to keep in touch with his followers who not only meant to support his case but also to 'convey to him the goods of your poor monastery, the which is like to be the impoverishment of your monastery if it continue any space'. The monks added that the abbot of Byland would presumably report to the king in a sense hostile to Rutland's intentions, in which surmise they were perfectly correct. They were very much afraid that Kirkby's deposition would yet be set aside: the rumour ran that the commission by whose authority he had been deprived was forged, that the only authority held by Legh and the commissioners was a mere letter from Cromwell, and that Cromwell was 'miscontented with Doctor Legh for his deed and says he shall repent it'. All this was very comforting to Kirkby's party and very heavy to Rutland's.

The earl seems to have forwarded this letter to Cromwell; there is no other reason for its appearance among the state papers. But Cromwell hardly needed such a reminder. The abbot of Byland's report, with its careful recitation of his commission and calm neglect of it in his doings, was sufficiently revealing. On 8 November 1533 the minister addressed one of his more formidable rockets to the abbots of Fountains and Byland, to remind them of their duty:[28]

After my full hearty manner I recommend me unto you. And whereas it hath pleased the king's highness to direct his most gracious letters unto you now at this present time for the election of a new abbot of Rievaulx, wherein his grace has been advertised ye have not heretofore endeavoured yourselves to the accomplishment of the same according to his said letters and commandment, whereof I marvel not a little that ye would incur his high displeasure for the non-executing of the same; therefore I heartily require and nevertheless do advise you, in eschewing of further inconveniences and displeasures that may thereby ensue, (all affections set apart) ye do accomplish the said election according to the tenor and purport of his most gracious letters directed unto you and to the convent of the same monastery in that behalf. And thereby ye shall not only deserve the king's most gracious thanks, but also have me to do for you in all your good causes the best I can.

Cromwell was master of a most effective epistolary style which preserved all the forms of politeness and gentle friendship while making plain the iron purpose beneath. The letter – threat, persuasion and promise rolled into one – did its work. The abbots 'set apart' their affection – an affection for their order rather than for Kirkby, one suspects – and on 10 December 1533 Thomas Legh could at last report that 'on St Nicholas Day [6 December] the abbot quondam of Rufford was installed at Rievaulx'.[29] Kirkby gave in: he exhibited his formal resignation to the commissioners, thereby removing the obstacle of an opposition party, and showed a conciliatory spirit by himself leading the singing of the *Te Deum* at the installation. His successor, Roland Blyton, had been translated from the Nottinghamshire monastery of Rufford; he was an elderly man whose appointment can be variously interpreted as an attempt to heal the split at Rievaulx or (less probably) as a long-term preparation for the dissolution of the house in which he was to co-operate willingly enough in 1538. Legh remarked in a postscript – with what truth we cannot tell – that 'all the country is glad of the new abbot and praise for them that helped thereto'.

Even so, Cromwell was not yet rid of Kirkby. In the letter in which he announced the end of the troubles at Rievaulx, Legh also mentioned the problem of providing for the deprived abbot. The commissioners decided to leave the settlement of a pension to the earl of Rutland, quite a proper step since the money would have to be found by 'his' monastery, but also a faintly malicious reminder that the position of patron could involve embarrassing responsibilities. Legh now showed another side to his character by strongly supporting Kirkby's claims.

> Although pity in all other things is good to be showed, yet it is most necessary in extremity or need; therefore I would he had an honest living, notwithstanding he has evil deserved it either to my said lord or me.

Perhaps it is not amiss at this point to recall that Kirkby would seem to have succeeded earlier in getting some favour with Cromwell as demonstrated by his acting as bearer for the second commission. Still, Legh's sentiments do him credit. For Cromwell it all meant further tiresome negotiations, for the new abbot proved unexpectedly obstinate about the pension. Very probably the earl did not forgive as readily as Dr Legh, so that no pressure was put on Blyton to provide for his predecessor. Direct dealings with him failed to produce results, and so Kirkby once more turned to Cromwell who finally supplied him with letters calling on the abbots of Fountains and Byland to arrange matters. By this time quite a few people must have wished that they had never heard of Edward Kirkby. On 28 May 1534 the two abbots acknowledged receipt of these fresh instructions and reported that they had held a meeting at Ripon on the 7th, having co-opted the abbot of Kirkstall as 'co-assistent' and calling before them the present and quondam abbots of Rievaulx.[30] After much discussion it was agreed that Kirkby should have an annual pension of £44 for life, the details to be arranged by the legal representatives of the two parties. The abbots noted with approval that Kirkby had abated higher claims, 'though, of very truth, there was more large sum of money offered . . . heretofore'. £44 was not a bad pension, though it may be compared with the 100 marks (£66. 13s. 4d.) which Blyton got when Rievaulx was dissolved.[31] However, when the deeds embodying this compromise had been got ready and were waiting to be sealed, Blyton began to make new delays. The abbots thought that 'the cause thereof is uncertain, and not a little we marvel that he keepeth not his said promise'. Perhaps the cause was Rutland, or simply dislike of burdening the monastery with so large an annual charge; perhaps internal politics were again involved. Manifestly annoyed with Blyton but unable to make him do the right thing, the abbots therefore passed the matter back to Cromwell.

At this Cromwell wrote sharply to Rievaulx and the papers were sealed, as appears from a reference in a later letter to 'a deed under your convent seal, which deed was sealed at the sight of my letters sent unto you'.[32] But this still produced no ready payments, and there followed a plentiful exchange of letters – only some of which are preserved and none of them dated – which it is impossible to sort out in proper sequence. Certainly Cromwell wrote several times to Blyton, and Kirkby more often still to Cromwell. In a very piteous epistle he revealed his ultimate ambitions by describing himself as abbot of Rievaulx, denying the justice of his deposition, and calling Cromwell his only hope.[33] He reminded the minister that he had earlier given Blyton the choice of either paying the pension or losing the abbacy, so that it seems that Cromwell had now turned round so far as to support Kirkby's claims to be restored. If he had changed sides so completely since the day that he obliged Rutland by securing Kirkby's removal, one may take this as further proof that no issue of politics or the king's interest was involved in the quondam's downfall. Kirkby went on to point out that the sitting abbot continued to ignore all letters sent to him, and that the time had therefore come for the threat to be put into operation. He promised to recompense Cromwell for his pains 'as shall be thought reasonable at your own taxation and judgment'. Some would no doubt see in this proffered bribe the reason for all Cromwell's efforts on Kirkby's behalf, but it is worth noting that Cromwell did not in fact restore Kirkby and also that it looks as though the offer was simply Kirkby's bright idea. The way in which it was phrased suggests strongly that earlier offers, naming a figure, had been made and ignored, and that the petitioner thought it a clever trick to suppose he could get better results by leaving Cromwell to fix his own price. Kirkby's letter proves that he thought Cromwell likely to follow the common practice of the day and expect to be well paid for his trouble; it does not prove that Cromwell in fact worked in that way or was so paid. There is no evidence at all that the many letters concerning Rievaulx which Cromwell wrote in the course of three years – amounting to a great deal of labour for a man as overworked as he was – ever earned him the slightest material advantage from anyone.

Under pressure from the minister, Blyton gave way. By the terms of the settlement reached on 7 May he was supposed to pay Kirkby's pension in two equal portions, one on 2 February (Purification of Our Lady: Candlemas) and the other on 1 August (St Peter ad Vincula: Lammas).[34] On 8 August 1534 Kirkby received his first instalment. But, as it happened, that was the end of it. For in the next session of Parliament (3 November – 18 December 1534) there was passed the act assigning the clerical first fruits and tenths to the crown.[35] By way of compensation to the new taxpayers, the statute limited the burden of pensions which rested on many ecclesiastical benefices. Section xx permitted all abbots who were paying to predecessors yet living pensions in excess of £40 p.a. to reduce these payments by half, all previous decisions and agreements to the contrary notwithstanding. As may be imagined, Blyton seized upon this escape clause with whoops of joy, and Candlemas 1535 passed without Kirkby receiving his due. In his extremity he again turned to Cromwell, but now the situation was very much altered. Even if he had wanted to, Cromwell could not override the tenor of the statute, and though Kirkby later maintained that a proper interpretation of the act would make it plain that it did not apply to his case, it is impossible to agree with him. Section xx very obviously and quite definitely cut his pension to £22.

Thus the second extant begging letter, written some time in 1535 and in Latin for better effect, had to overcome novel difficulties.[36] Kirkby had to begin by admitting that Cromwell had told him several times to stop bothering him with his concerns. Having failed to gain access to Cromwell's 'egregia persona', the indefatigable suitor persuaded the minister's nephew Richard to forward his new petition. The issue had now narrowed to that half of the pension which Blyton declared he was statutorily absolved from paying. Kirkby remarked that if that was the case he would utterly perish, but to him it appeared 'luce clarius' that the act bore no such meaning. Unfortunately, his mere assertion did not make it so. Since 8 August he had had not a penny from Blyton and was living on the charity of his friends. To ease Cromwell's labours he added a draft letter in English which sternly reminded Blyton of his commitment and warned him that Kirkby would be restored to Rievaulx unless the full pension were paid. The letter differs from Cromwell's genuine ones by being much more abrupt and openly hostile, though there are several phrases to testify to the care with which Kirkby had studied the minister's earlier letters. Cromwell was made to remark on Blyton's failure to pay, 'whereof I do marvel'; there was a reference to the possibility that 'I assure you, I can no less do in good conscience and equity than to find some means to restore him to his abbacy again, like as I have heretofore written to you'; the letter ended on a not uncharacteristically ominous note – if Blyton would 'list to ruffle any further in the matter, thinking that this my advertisement is not for your ease, do as ye think best'. Nevertheless, it was not a letter of Cromwell's, and despite Kirkby's request for his *imprimatur* it never became one. The services of Richard Cromwell did not suffice to persuade his uncle once more to take a hand in the matter, especially now that the statute supported Blyton. Cromwell had secured Kirkby his pension in the teeth of strong opposition. If now, by act of Parliament, that pension was cut in half there was nothing he could do and certainly nothing he would do. It is even possible that in drafting the act he had been influenced by memories of the representations of poverty and inability to pay heavy pensions which must have reached him from Rievaulx when he pressed Kirkby's claim earlier in the year. But this instance of poetic injustice is necessarily conjectural.

For the moment Kirkby disappears from sight, no doubt living on £22 a year as best he might. It was not an impossible sum – monastic pensions after the Dissolution for all but abbots rarely exceeded £10 – but after his income at Rievaulx it represented real hardship. Thus the Pilgrimage of Grace came as an obvious opportunity for him to recover his fortunes. Characteristically he tried to play on both sides, but with little success. The full story cannot be known: all we have is a letter to Cromwell from the duke of Norfolk, the king's lieutenant in the north, written on 3 October 1537, after the troubles were over.[37] From this it emerges that Kirkby had at first hoped to gain his ends from the rebels. Norfolk accused him of having 'showed himself in the times of the late business as false and traitorous an heart as any in these quarters'. But unlike so many he managed to avoid the worst consequences, and by October 1537 he was once again assailing Blyton from the winning side. Norfolk had been shown a citation ordering Blyton's appearance in 'the court' to answer for the fact that he had without right or title entered upon the abbacy of Rievaulx although that monastery was then not vacant. What court is meant is obscure. A citation issued from an ecclesiastical court, so that perhaps the court of the archbishop of York was in question. On the other hand, Norfolk thought that the summons had been obtained under Cromwell's authority, which suggests the possibility that a conciliar instrument may have been used – either Star Chamber or some otherwise unknown juridical authority exercised by Cromwell as vicegerent in spirituals. Norfolk went on, one feels without much need:

> I doubt not but ye know right well of the sending down of the king's highness' commission into these parts to remove the said quondam, about a three years past, for such misorder as he used within the said monastery.

He pleaded that Blyton was too old to be well able to ride

and moreover 'of as honest a sort as any one religious man
in these parts', and therefore begged Cromwell to excuse
him the personal appearance demanded by the citation.
If Kirkby persisted in his suit, Blyton might be permitted
to answer by his counsel (proctor), as was proper. Cromwell was also to take no notice if Kirkby charged Blyton
with failing to pay his pension, 'for he did the same by my
commandment given unto him immediately after the
said quondam was first suspected of treason'. The duke's
intercession was a very strong card in Blyton's hand and
would have ended Kirkby's chances even if he had not
temporarily been implicated in the rebellion. He spent
six weeks in the Tower and was even rumoured to have
suffered execution together with his old friend, Thirsk of
Fountains Abbey, but in the end he escaped.[38] He survived to lay by his ambitions, to see his monastery put
down, and as a parish priest to serve God as best he might
in the many changes that came upon the Church of
England before his death in 1557.

There remains one larger issue in which it is possible
that Abbot Edward's tribulations played an unsuspected
part. It has always seemed a little odd (at least to me) that
the Act of Supremacy of 1534,[39] which in the main did no
more than confirm that the king was supreme head of the
Church of England and as such possessed of all the rights
and profits attached to that dignity, should have gone out
of its way to define and confer just one of these rights:

And that our said sovereign lord ... shall have full
power and authority from time to time to visit, repress,
redress, reform, order, correct, restrain and amend all
such errors, heresies, abuses, offences, contempts and
enormities ... which by any manner spiritual authority and jurisdiction ought or may lawfully be re-

formed . . . : any usage, custom, foreign laws, foreign authority, prescription or other thing or things to the contrary hereof notwithstanding.

We remember the difficulties experienced in May 1533 when abbots of the Cistercian order employed the rules of their religion to hamper or even thwart an inchoate attempt to enforce a royal visitatorial authority which was at the time far from well defined; and we remember Cromwell's customary preference for statutory authority in all he did or attempted to do. Is it not possible that when he came to consider the Act of Supremacy he recalled Abbot Edward Kirkby and the problem of removing him from Rievaulx, and that this memory was at least in part responsible for this detailed statutory elaboration of an authority which it could well be argued was in any case fully comprehended in the general confirmation of rights and powers which preceded it?

But perhaps the story received its final touch of crowning irony in March 1539 when the king granted the lands of the lately dissolved monastery of Rievaulx, in exchange for some other lands, to Thomas Manners, earl of Rutland.[40] Like many others, founders and patrons, the earl had at last discovered a way of turning patronage and distant interference into the most direct form of control.

6

TITHE AND TROUBLE

An anticlerical story

The story of the war waged by the villagers of Hayes in Middlesex against their parish clergy provides, on the very eve of the Reformation, a splendid case history to test the well-known commonplace that the Reformation was successful in England because the country was resolutely anticlerical – because people disliked priests and hated the claims and the courts of the Church. Hayes may now be a London suburb; in 1530 it was a village in the shire, remaining so as late as the middle of the nineteenth century when it was regarded as 'the most backward part of the county'.[1] It comprised a manor whose lord was the archbishop of Canterbury; that see had allegedly acquired it as early as 832.[2] The archbishop also owned the advowson, the right to present to the living. In consequence the parish was a 'peculiar' of Canterbury, that is to say it was exempt from the bishop of London's jurisdiction and came directly under the archbishop's.[3] The village was therefore just a little out of the ordinary: it lay near London, and it enjoyed a direct relationship with the primate of England. These facts, as will become

174

apparent, had something to do with the troubles which
beset it in the later 1520s, but they do not make so much
difference that one need regard Hayes as altogether
exceptional.

The archbishop of the day was William Warham who
had been elevated to Canterbury in 1503, largely for the
services in diplomacy and the law he had rendered to
Henry VII. He had had no rapid career – on his accession
to the see he was already about fifty-two years old – but
was to survive until 1532, a thorn in Wolsey's side. In
1515 he abandoned his office of lord chancellor to the
rising star and retired to the duties of the archbishopric.
Of these the affairs of Hayes were a small part which need
never have come to his grace's personal attention if he had
not bestowed the rectory on a favourite – his relative,
namesake and archdeacon William Warham who occupied
it from 1516 till his death in 1557.[4] 'Occupied', however,
is not quite the right word, for this other William
Warham, sufficiently busy with his archidiaconical duties
at Canterbury, found it necessary to appoint a vicar to
look after the souls of Hayes while he himself collected
the revenues of the rectory, including the tithe. Not that
there was anything unusual in this arrangement: by the
later middle ages few rectories in England could rely on
the services of an active incumbent. By 1520 Warham
had persuaded his august relative to ordain a vicarage at
Northwood Chapel, served by a chaplain appointed by the
vicar who himself served the parish church at Hayes,
unless he too appointed a further deputy.[5] It may be – it
would be interesting to know more about this – that the
population of the region was rising; there is some evidence
of population increases at this time, and London and its
environs might well have been early affected. At any rate,
Warham claimed that the work had got too much for one

priest, so that now the clergy of Hayes consisted of an absentee rector, a vicar in the parish church, and a curate at Northwood.

At this point, the archdeacon introduced a further complication. At some date after 1520 he came to the conclusion that his income from Hayes was not worth the trouble of direct collection and let the rectory to farm. The first farmer was one John Osborne of whom nothing more is known; the second a certain Thomas Gold, a lawyer of the Middle Temple.[6] As the sequel was to show, the lease included all the profits of the rectory, more especially the tithe; much later, Gold estimated the income at £100 a year, but that was pretty certainly an exaggeration flung out under stress and by way of a grievance.[7] Gold soon brought in a new vicar, only the second in line; following the example set by his manorial lord he, too, practised nepotism and picked his brother Henry. Henry Gold has some claims to recognition in his own right. He had a distinguished enough career at Cambridge, becoming a fellow of St. John's College in 1516 and remaining there certainly until early 1525, though he never progressed beyond his master's degree.[8] That he had familiar contacts with Thomas More's circle as early as 1514 also argues well for his scholarly interests.[9] But while pursuing an academic career he kept his eye on the important chance of ecclesiastical preferment and with his brother attached himself to the entourage of Archbishop Warham: by 1519 he had obtained the honour and benefit of a chaplaincy.[10] His fuller reward came in 1526, when he was collated to the benefice of St Mary Aldermanbury in the city of London, also one of the archbishop's peculiars.[11] City livings were normally fine prizes to win, but this one unfortunately carried the burden of a £30 pension to the previous incumbent, and

Gold must therefore have found the offer of Hayes attractive – the more attractive since it was additional to his benefice in London which he does not appear to have resigned.[12] All this time Warham also employed his chaplain in various legal business; Thomas, too, cashed in on the family connection when he obtained letters of attorney from the archbishop in a common law matter.[13] So far, then, Henry had pursued the ordinary course of the intelligent and successful clerical careerist: university don, chaplain to a great man, preferred to a handsome living, promoted to pluralism. If the villagers of Hayes were unusually lucky in getting a vicar of some learning, they might also from the start wonder why so fashionable a man should come to their village, and they might well foresee the absences in which his pluralism involved him. The arrival as farmer of the rectory, and especially of its tithes, of a London lawyer was certainly a matter fraught with ominous possibilities.

It seems that Gold knew what he was up against, for the village had a record of conflict. When, after the troubles to be related here, he at length succeeded in having his adversaries sent to the Fleet by the court of Star Chamber, he mentioned, among other things, that they had also ill-treated Henry Gold's predecessor as vicar, so much so that he was glad to be quit of the parish. The accused did not deny the old vicar's difficulties but alleged that his enemies had not been of their number but one Robert Kyng, a leading supporter of Thomas Gold's, and John Osborne who had farmed the rectory before Gold. They themselves had in fact tried to help the vicar.[14] Quite possibly they were telling the truth; there is much internal village strife behind the story that can be discovered, and it would be reasonable to suppose that Gold had been misled by his supporters, or even that we have here a twisted echo of the Gold brothers' manœuvres in getting hold of farm and vicarage.

Gold's own troubles arose from a quarrel over tithe; they developed into a double attack on the villagers, conducted by the archbishop in the ecclesiastical courts and the farmer in the secular courts; they finished up with Gold's appeal to Star Chamber where, as usual, the matter peters out with no hope of establishing the court's decision. More than fifteen documents, most of them long, have had to be used to sort out the facts and their sequence; constant reference to them would make the story less intelligible rather than more. The reconstruction has to bring together evidence which is now unreasonably scattered throughout the Star Chamber records; it will be best to append a list here and to cite the documents hereafter only if it should seem desirable to do so.[15] This great mass of paper reflects a strenuous and bitter quarrel; its bulk is the more impressive when it appears that the disputes lasted for little more than a year.

For a time there was something like a state of open war in the village. On the one side stood the rector and vicar, brothers in blood and brothers in arms, assisted by the curate (or parish priest, as he is called) Peter Lee, by the parish clerk Thomas Troughton, by Gold's farm-labourers and by a small group in the village the chief of whom were Robert Kyng, a substantial man in his middle fifties, his son Richard (twenty-five), Roger Hopwood (forty) who kept a tavern, and two young men just turned twenty, Robert Wapull and Gregory Faxton. According to the other party, all these men were highly unsatisfactory characters.[16] Some of them had before this been amerced for misbehaviour in the parish, and Gold had paid their fines so as to secure their services as witnesses. Troughton had been 'for his evil demeanour . . .

warned out of his office' by the churchwardens, but Gold
kept him on, even though he had first led the attack on the
clerk whom he only supported when he could use him
against the parish. Robert Kyng had never been in favour
with his neighbours; Hopwood 'kept ill rule in his house,
both dicing and carding with vagabonds' – though this
charge must be read against Gold's earlier allegation of
the same thing against the village; another man was 'a
suspect person, as is known in the county'. Parson Lee
was 'suspected with the wife of the said Hopwood' with
whom he had allegedly spent some days at Mrs Daws'
house in Honey Lane Ward in London before being
warned off by the ward constable; Mrs Daws, with other
women 'suspect of misliving', had been turned out of
Hayes after a visit there. Lee had also broken a man's
head in a quarrel in church and had further 'come into the
street at unlawful hours in the night, sometimes barefoot
and barelegged, with his bow in his hand and an arrow in
it, to the intent to do displeasure to some of the parishioners'. Gold had disobeyed an order from the archbishop to dismiss him. Faxton was 'but a vagabond and
useth no craft nor occupation, nor hath no certain
dwelling place, nor no man knoweth whereupon he
liveth'. Wapull, in service to Gold, was used as an *agent
provocateur* against the villagers, 'giving them occasion to
break the king's peace to the intent that they should break
their recognisance of good bearing'. It looks as though
Gold stepped straight into an old quarrel between neighbours (in which the Church had already become involved)
and made it worse by his eagerness to exploit the rectory
financially. Even before Gold leased the farm, Archdeacon
Warham had sued some of the parish in the ecclesiastical
courts, apparently without success (the issue was compromised) but leaving a legacy of vociferous grievances.[17]

The party opposed to Gold seems to have included the bulk of the parish; on more than one occasion they described themselves, and were described by others, as the inhabitants of Hayes *par excellence*. Quite a few people got involved in the troubles, but the leaders were Thomas Bradley, a forceful man of some substance, turned forty; William Rowse, a few years older, constable of the parish; Nicholas Kyng (fifty), perhaps related to the misliked Robert but very definitely on the other side; William Stevyn the younger, a man just over twenty who, in company with his friend Michael Harding, acted as spearhead for Bradley's attacks on Gold; and two other men, Nicholas Vincent and John Nicolls. All these were native to Hayes; there was in addition a group of citizens of London who got mixed up in the business. Henry Kyng and his son Matthew may have been related to Nicholas, but Henry Greenwood (a clothworker) and George Wryght are less easily connected. They may all have been Gold's enemies in London rather than Hayes; the farmer was after all a Middle Temple lawyer and spent much of his time looking after his affairs in the city. On the other hand, all these four Londoners attended mass at Hayes on Whitmonday 1530, though no one can now say whether they did so because they were visiting friends and relations or because they had come to join hands with Bradley and Rowse in a preconcerted action against the Golds. It is quite impossible to disentangle the true position completely: as things stand, we are unusually lucky to be granted so much insight into these quarrels between groups of neighbours on the one hand and between the parish and its ecclesiastical authorities on the other. The two quarrels may just have coalesced; or there may have been only the one issue of tithe and offerings leading to the formation of parties. What is certain is that the payments to the Church and the activities of the lay farmer of the rectory and his priestly brother precipitated the real troubles.

Tithe, certainly, lay at the heart of the issue. What we know about it in detail relates to the harvest of 1530; but there were battles between Gold and Bradley throughout that year, and some of the evidence suggests that Gold had upset the village at the previous year's harvest. Since Henry Gold did not become vicar until December 1529, Thomas must have leased the rectory some time before he could get the vicarage for his brother. However, 1530 was the critical year. Gold charged Bradley with being 'the chief causer of the said great offences, misdemeanours and contempts'.[18] By threats and persuasion he had stopped his fellows from laying out their tithe corn, and since Easter 1530 he had prevented the parish from making any oblations at marriages, churchings, burials and the like, 'contrary to their old laudable customs to the great hurt and damages of the said Thomas Gold'. Lee confirmed that offerings had indeed fallen away; when, for instance, William Andrew was married on 25 September 1530 all present withdrew at the critical moment and he got paid only by the bridal pair. When the time came to make collection, Bradley and his friends would commonly 'laugh and make great game openly in the said church'.[19] All this was confirmed by Gold's other witnesses;[20] Wapull said he heard Bradley say that the vicar was to have 'no more fools' farthings . . . to sue them with in the law'.

Matters came to a head with the harvest. Gold alleged that the villagers refused to lay out their tithe sheaves until they had carried their own corn, which was contrary to custom, and that after their corn had been moved he had had twenty-six loads standing neglected in one field. The villagers had then calmly let their beasts on to the stubble, so that his servants had removed seventy-nine head of cattle and horses ('besides hogs') one morning, and some twenty to thirty a day after that for three weeks, all of whom were destroying his corn. He claimed further loss through deceitful tithing. These charges were backed up by William Patterson, his carter, Roger Chamley, who pitched for him, and Robert Till who sometimes gathered and sometimes pitched. Patterson had seen one of the villagers take away eighty sheaves without leaving any tithe corn; another, who should have laid out twenty-five, only presented thirteen. He reckoned Gold had lost twenty marks 'what in one place and other' by illegal carrying, and £20 'what the last year and this year' by untrue tithing. The other men told similar stories of cheating and gave details of the cattle they had chased off, but would not estimate the losses.[21]

Gold maintained that half-way through the harvest Bradley had persuaded the villagers to break the old custom of separating the rector's share (every tenth sheaf) at the binding 'or shocking' and to change over to the pernicious practice of first carting their corn so that the rector would have great difficulty both in checking his tithe and in having it carried. Several villagers, belonging (it seems) to neither party, were asked about this.[22] Robert Foot, an old man of sixty-eight, admitted that he had changed his practice, but he gave a reason which, though it involved Bradley, also reflected on Gold. He had called Bradley over, as that worthy was passing by during the harvest, to tell him that Gold 'had been with him and asked him why he would not tithe as he was wont to do', to which Foot had replied, 'he would tithe well enough and that he should have the tenth sheaf'. Bradley's advice was that Foot 'should not need to lay out his tithe corn until he had carried away his corn'. Robert Kyng, who like Gold's other witnesses deposed to the old custom, asserted that Foot had told him he had changed his practice because Bradley rebuked him, but in this instance a partisan statement can for once be checked against one from a neutral source, and the result does not encourage too firm a belief in Gold's witnesses. Another peasant, George Flee, said he had changed his method because it was reported 'that when the said Gold's cart came for his tithe his cattle did eat and despoil their corn, and also if they that came with his cart or other his gatherers did mislike his tithe sheaf they would set up that that was laid out for the tithe and take a better'. Annoyed by such high-handedness, he and his neighbours had decided to carry their own corn first. These and others denied intimidation by Bradley, but William Parke stated that he acted as charged because Bradley said to him: 'But if thou wilt [not] break that custom of tithing at the binding and lay out no tithe till the carrying, as we do in the parish here, thou shalt dwell no longer in this town.' Edmund Cope had heard Bradley and Rowse agree before the harvest that the tithe should no longer be put out and to stop others from doing so, and Troughton had overheard a similar conversation while drinking at Rowse's house. At that time one Witchington had revealed that he had agreed with Gold about his tithe on Gold's terms, for which Rowse called him 'a knave, a wretch and a devil, to do otherwise than his neighbours would do'.

The issue was one familiar to anyone who has ever looked into the cumbersome and complicated law of tithe.* Praedial tithes – those payable on the fruits of the

---

* For a detailed and excellent recent account of tithe, though admittedly after the Reformation (which made little difference) see C. Hill, *Economic Problems of the Church from Whitgift to Laud* (1956), 78 ff.

earth and increase of animals, the only ones here in dispute – entitled the parson to every tenth sheaf harvested and every tenth beast born.[23] It was normal practice to set aside the corn tithe so that the parson could see fair distribution done; 'but if the custom of the place be otherwise the parson must sit down by it'.[24] Beasts were more difficult because they refused to turn up in handy lots of ten. Normally, payment was held over till ten lambs or calves had been born; if the owner sold the beasts he owed the parson a tenth of the money made. Everything depended on custom, the custom of the parish. When, after the break with Rome and especially after the dissolution of the monasteries, the owners of tithe (both lay and ecclesiastical) found ever greater difficulty in extorting their rights, Parliament intervened with statutes which declared tithe lawful, ordered any 'immemorial' (forty-years old) custom in its payment to be observed, and brought in the secular arm (the king's Council, the justice of the peace) to enforce it.[25] The practice of cheating the parson by carrying the corn before he had had a chance of viewing it was sufficiently widespread for the Parliament of 1548 to impose specific penalties on it. The villagers of Hayes were not alone in their tricks, but they had unquestionably put themselves in the wrong by abandoning custom: all the witnesses, even those who were not wedded to Gold's party, agreed that the customary procedure had been abandoned. Bradley claimed that some people had always used the new way, but he mentioned only one man by name, and that a rabid supporter of his.[26] He also denied having used persuasion or threats to others, but it can hardly be doubted that he did.

It is not surprising, therefore, that when the parish in their turn wished to accuse Gold of having upset customary arrangements they ignored corn and concentrated on

beasts.[27] 'Of a great, ancient and continuance whereof no
mind of man is', the terms of tithe at Hayes (apart from
that on wool and grain) had been the tenth calf and lamb,
a halfpenny being paid for every 'odd lamb' under seven;
if the beasts to be tithed were seven exactly, the parson
got one of them and a halfpenny for each up to ten thereafter; for animals sold he got a tithe of the purchase
money. Some thirty years earlier there had apparently
been sufficient dispute for the matter to be referred to
arbitration at a very high level; a commission which
included Thomas Jane (bishop of Norwich), Thomas
Ruthal (later bishop of Durham) and John Yonge (later
master of the rolls) had confirmed these customs. In those
days the parson was satisfied and the parish 'well and
sufficiently instructed, with good wholesome spiritual
doctrine for the soul's health'. This idyllic peace was
shattered when Dr Warham leased the rectory to Gold
who 'is something learned in the law and a man desirous
of trouble and the vexation of his poor neighbours'. In
matters of tithe he wished to change the custom, demanding that odd animals should be left over till the year after;
he would not take money because he thought 'the having
of every such beast is more to his advantage', an attitude
which correctly reflects rising prices and the inadequacy
of ancient compositions. Moreover, at harvest time he
would come round with three of four armed men, and if
the tithe corn set aside was not to his liking he would help
himself to other corn from the villagers' sheaves. These
are only some of his troublesome deeds cited in the
complaint, but they are the only ones that concern tithe. It
does not look as though Gold had done very much wrong,
though William Rowse also stressed that the change in
carting corn was made when Gold's servants began high-
handedly to reject the tithe corn and take some the men

had set aside for themselves. Experiencing difficulties in collecting his fair share of the harvest, Gold seems to have taken rather tactless measures which proved the last straw to the villagers. Gold was unpopular, probably grasping, certainly given to standing on his rights; the village retaliated by moving the harvest before he could establish what was his due.

If tithe and other payments were the first cause of the quarrel, other and less ecclesiastical issues also arose to trouble the peace. While Bradley could be accused of depriving the Church of its income, Rowse could be charged with keeping a house of little order and with neglecting his duty. Apart from his office of constable, Rowse seems also to have kept some sort of tavern. At least, his house was one much resorted to for drinking, and although the licensing of inns was somewhat uncertain at this date it is probable that he kept at least a wineshop, if not a proper hostelry. Gold not only denounced his house as the centre of plots against himself, but also claimed that people habitually ate and drank there during the hours of divine service and at times played unlawful games, like cards and dice and tennis, with shedding of blood.[28] This was thoroughly and convincingly elaborated by his witnesses. Lee, as usual most detailed in his depositions, charged several parishioners with missing all or part of mass because they were too busy playing. He and others spoke feelingly of the heavy gambling and high stakes common at the house; Bradley, who had been poor when he first came to Hayes, had now achieved 'good substance' by his organized gaming. Two men, Thomas Tanner and William Jackett, had lost everything, sold their land, and were now in penury, all because of Bradley's winning streak. Tanner himself, unfortunately for this sad story, would only say that he and others had often played there but that he knew of no one undone thereby. One Edward Romen allegedly had been so reduced by his gambling losses that he 'did counterfeit the king's coins and was taken and committed to Newgate, and remained there by a long season and was examined thereof'; Romen's own deposition has nothing of this, and one may add that if he had been taken for coining he would have been very unlikely to come alive from Newgate.[29]

It was further alleged that Rowse had failed to prevent unlawful outdoor games, as tennis, bowls, quoits, football; worse still, the playing of these games had been accompanied by betting and bloodshed. Witnesses spoke of seeing men fight at football, of bloody noses and mouths, and always the men to the fore were people like Bradley, Stevyn, Rowse and his fellow-constable Osmond – all the leaders of the opposition. Or else, to see the thing in the round, the leaders of the village, for even if we do not take the contemptuous description of Gold's followers at its face value it still remains plain that he had no adherents beyond those tied to him by interest. Still, if Lee was right and the constables had never done anything to stop illegal games, had never presented anyone at the court leet for engaging in them or for any of the minor offences arising from hot blood at football and the like (and Lee claimed to have this direct from the archbishop's officers responsible for holding this lesser criminal court), it could not be denied that Rowse was not doing his duty. No doubt he was in a position only too familiar to village constables at the time and he will not have taken kindly to the rector's farmer when this newcomer kept telling him to take steps against his friends and neighbours; but the charge was one which would look well in the court of Star Chamber. Both he and Bradley stoutly denied that anything improper went on at his house. The place was

commonly used by the people of the neighbouring
hamlets to drink and break their fast after morning mass,
but any meetings held there were just for making merry.
Nor had either of them heard of any trouble at the outdoor
games which, as they admitted, the young men occasionally played.[30]

Gold later produced against Rowse one specific charge
of dereliction of duty. On 25 May 1530, Agnes Gold,
Thomas's wife, allegedly appealed to the constable to
arrest a certain Richard Page 'for certain causes and misdemeanours that she knew in him', but though Rowse did
at first arrest him he let him escape a few hours later. The
fuller story told by the witnesses is less straightforward.
Mrs Gold laid her information in church, secretly but in
Page's presence. Rowse, for the malice that he bore to the
Golds, at once disclosed 'that counsel' by saying loudly:
'God's body, come hither, man, come hither and answer
for thyself, for she will make thee a thief.' Page turned
furiously upon the informer, pushed her with hands and
elbows, threatened her with the stick he carried, and
growled: 'What am I? What knowest thou by me? What
wilt thou make me?' Mrs Gold was so disconcerted by
these threats that she 'remained in worse health of her
body . . . by a long time after', but not so much as to omit
to charge Rowse once more to arrest Page as a 'naughty
and misruled person', which he then did. Some few hours
later Page came to see Lee and asked for his company to
the vicarage and his help in begging Agnes Gold to withdraw the charge. Lee complied. When they got there,
Page said that William Rowse had told him of the charge
but that he himself had not heard her say any such words.
She stoutly replied that Rowse was right. Page turned to
entreaty: he was a gentleman born, and unless she dropped
the matter 'he should be shamed and all his blood'. If she

pressed the charge he would be undone for ever, for the constable – who had incidentally taken a bond for £100 off him before letting him go to see her – 'would else have him to Mr Chesman, a justice of the peace'. This is told by Lee, who was present, and it would seem to exonerate rather than burden the constable.

Lee also explained how Page had roused suspicion: he had certainly behaved oddly enough. We are told just enough to wish to know more of one who may well have been a colourful rogue. A stranger and unknown to anyone in Hayes, Page had spent a few days at Rowse's house (which, it is well to recall, may have been an inn); yet 'no reasonable cause could be there known why he should so resort thither'. During his stay, he had one day 'suddenly and secretly' entered the houses of Thomas Burbage and Thomas Gold during these gentlemen's absence, had walked all round the hall and parlour and other rooms 'without any speaking or knocking', had thoroughly surveyed the houses and the ground round them, and had departed without a word of explanation, leaving the households in fear, doubt and perturbation. To add to the suspicion that he was a felon spying out the land, he called himself Page to some and Payne to others and gave different home addresses in London, as St Magnus' parish or the Dove in Friday Street or Cheapside. He had an injured hand which he explained by a story of a fight with Alderman Partridge who had allegedly refused to sell him a hogshead of wine, whereas Mr Partridge had in fact died some three or four years earlier. Moreover, there seemed a chance that he had been involved in a robbery lately committed in Mr Chesman's house: he was known to have paid visits to a dwelling nearby before he came to Hayes and was thought to have lurked 'in woods and hedgerows' just before the robbery.

To this charge that he had let a prisoner escape, Rowse thought he had a perfect answer. He admitted that Agnes Gold accused Page of being a 'naughty fellow', and that Page stayed at his house for a few days, but maintained that she never formally charged him with felony so that he never had him in his constabulary custody. This, if Lee's story was true, approximated to a quibble, for Page clearly thought himself more or less under arrest and in danger of the justice of the peace – moreover the very justice whom he was suspected of robbing; also the £100 bond could be used against Rowse as proving that he had Page in custody and was no doubt for that reason sworn to by Lee. Yet Rowse could argue – as he did – that it had never got to a formal charge, so that his taking Page away with him from the church and later taking a bond from him were merely precautionary measures in case the charge should yet be laid. On this point, for once, Gold does not seem to have the law entirely on his side.[31]

However, what really matters in all this is the picture of disturbances and quarrels which is presented. Quite clearly the village was fairly united against the farmer and the vicar who for support relied almost only on their servants, and the leading villagers took pleasure in egging the young men on against these unimpressive representatives of the spirituality. Young William Stevyn, for one, often quarrelled loudly with Gold,[32] though the only words recorded are somewhat obscure in import: 'He knew the law as well as the same Gold did; and that the cat of the said Gold did kitten before her time, and that his cat kittened in her time, and that he would not give one kitling thereof for a noble; and also . . . that the said Gold leapt over the stile or [before] he came at it.' If precipitancy was all that could be laid at Gold's door, the village had less cause to complain than it made issue of. Michael

Harding – who, though he appears several times in the story, was never called upon to answer for himself – had been rather ruder in refusing to pay a debt, on 21 November 1530: 'Thy master,' he had told Gold's servant, 'getteth no money of me and that I will try with him by Stafford law', with 'other unfitting words' which, according to one deponent, were 'the devil's turd in thy master's teeth'. 'Stafford law' is a happy phrase for the code of the stronger, the use of staves; though it is not entirely unknown elsewhere, this would appear to be the earliest example vouched for since the *Oxford Diction-ary* cannot find it before the Marprelate Tracts of 1589.

There seems to be some truth also in the story that the Golds were trying hard to suborn witnesses; certainly the parish clerk was mentioned in one place as one of the obstreperous young men and yet gave evidence on Gold's behalf. He even turned upon a benefactor when he revealed how Rowse had once advised him in a scrape.[33] Having been cited in the archbishop's court of the Arches for calling a woman a whore, he had taken Rowse's advice. When Rowse was told that no one else had heard him use the word complained of, he told Troughton to deny the charge 'whatsoever betide'. Rowse had also encouraged Troughton at one time to stand up to Gold, promising him that no harm should come to him; but now Troughton told all and by his change of sides gave colour to the villagers' accusation that Gold was bribing men, one way or another, to bear witness against his enemies.

By the second half of 1530 things had got to such a pass that Bradley and his friends (though of course they denied it) habitually drifted over to the vicarage after service, to pick a quarrel with the Golds.[34] Their language was allegedly lurid: 'cankered churl and cankered knave', 'I am as good a gentleman as thou art, and the king, I tell thee, can make no gentlemen', 'he was but a penny gentleman and . . . a false knave'. This suggests that Thomas Gold, that London lawyer, was giving himself airs. The vicar was called 'knave priest and polled priest'. They threatened never to stop baiting them till they had baited them out of the town. Those Sunday scenes, with the rector and vicar scurrying home from church while a jeering crowd yapped at their heels, must have been edifying in the extreme. The talk was that if only the village stuck together the two brothers 'should not be able to abide it': Bradley and Rowse hoped to drive them from Hayes by making life intolerable for them. They little knew Thomas Gold's temper, and they also seem to have overlooked the resources of the law. But for this last they had some excuse, for these scenes came only at the end of several months during which Gold tried in vain to use both the common and the canon law against his enemies. In Hayes the year 1530 witnessed a succession of legal processes attempted against the ringleaders of the village and shrugged off by them with ease and contempt. The actions were a mingling of Gold's endeavours to recover debts or goods withheld from him, and of the archbishop's endeavours to get him his tithe.

The first recorded clash took place on 16 January 1530 when two royal bailiffs (Robert Francis and Thomas Dixon), together with the archbishop's bailiff of the manor (Walter Hunt), tried to serve a *non omittas* on Nicholas Kyng. But the nature of that writ makes certain that earlier steps had in fact been taken. The writ of *non omittas* was meant to help those who had tried in vain to get justice in a liberty through the officers of the owner of that liberty. As Gold explained,[35] he had failed to get earlier writs served by the archbishop's officers, for Hayes was not only a Canterbury manor and a Canterbury peculiar, but Canterbury had there also franchisal rights of jurisdiction. He therefore intended to avail himself of the royal writ devised to break through the obstinacy, or to make up for the weakness, of private bailiffs; hence the *non omittas*, though what he wanted from Nicholas Kyng is never made clear, and in fact the day chosen was a bad one because Kyng was then away from Hayes.[36] At any rate, it proved a bad day for Dixon. When he rode into the yard of the alehouse kept by Roger Hopwood he was met by Michael Harding who started mocking him, saying his horse 'should bear a gentleman out of town'. Dixon at first replied peaceably enough that he was no gentleman and his horse was good enough for him, until Harding sneered that in that case the horse should carry a knave out of town. At this Dixon got hot: 'he would try that with him if he were off his horse'. Harding promptly pulled him off and set about him, and the bailiff had very much the worse of the exchange. The fight attracted a crowd, some running off to fetch weapons; some others held Francis back as he tried to come to his colleague's assistance; George Osmond, one of the constables, used Dixon's own sword to keep others from breaking up the fight. Peter Lee, who was watching from the vicarage window, saw the villagers form a ring round the struggling men; it reminded him of nothing so much as of the scene at a cockfight. The battle did not last long: Nicholas Vincent, who had gone to get himself a cudgel, was disappointed to find it over on his return and explained that if he could have been back quicker the bailiff 'should have borne him two or three blows'. William Stevyn panted up too late from playing football and also expressed his regret; his aggressive posture nearly revived the affray. However, Dixon was allowed to depart and nurse his bruises. A number of the more ardent spirits then made a hero out of Harding; they 'had him to the alehouse and there spent their money upon him and made him great cheer' for 'the best deed that ever he did in Hayes'.[37]

There can be no question that this fight took place; even Gold's enemies had to admit it, though Bradley, Rowse and Nicolls explained that at the time they were with Thomas Gold valuing 'certain stuff of the old vicar's' and knew these things only by report. The description given of it does not sound so very terrible: there was no concerted rush, no attempt to kill, only a goodhumoured forming of a ring and letting the two fighting cocks get on with it. When Dixon had had enough he was allowed to go, and after all he had asked for the fight. The trouble was that a king's officer had been beaten and the law frustrated. According to Gold's witnesses, this 'victory' encouraged wild and rather silly talk in the village, to the effect that 'it is no offence to slay or kill a bailiff or summoner and that there is no law nor punishment therefor'. It was proving more and more impossible to serve any process in the village. Apart from the occasions still to be described in detail, there was trouble as late as 30 April 1531 (by which time the Star Chamber had a hand in things) when William Stevyn and Nicholas Vincent abused Walter Hunt and Robert Kyng for trying to serve a writ of *withernam* on Stevyn.* On that occasion others prevented violence – Nicholas Spurling held Vincent back

* Doc. D. *Withernam* was served upon the failure of a *replevin*, and a *replevin* had been tried on Stevyn in June 1530 (cf. below, p. 198). All these writs were stages in the process of recovering goods withheld from plaintiff: if X had distrained goods from Y for alleged damages, Y could use *replevin* to recover his goods on condition that he bound himself to meet X's grievances at law; and if *replevin* failed *withernam* would order the sheriff to take an equivalent quantity of X's goods as Y's security till the action be settled.

with the words 'what will ye do? Remember what case ye stand in. Let us go and drink a pot of ale at Rowse's' — but the writ was not served. Contempt for the law and its servants was growing apace in Hayes. It may not have been a new feature — the lot of bailiffs and process-servers is proverbially hard — but it was a feature which Star Chamber would not lightly let pass.

The ball next passed to the archbishop. On 6 June 1530, in response to Thomas Gold's complaint that the parishioners would not pay their tithe and other dues, Warham sent his apparitor, Thomas Dodworth, to cite certain of them before his court 'for causes of reformation of their souls'. This provoked a riot. Four citizens of London (Henry Kyng, Matthew Kyng, Henry Greenwood and George Wryght) and one native of Hayes (William Stevyn) 'violently and riotously in the parish church . . . nothing regarding nor honouring the mass nor the holy sacrament which was then there said and consecrate nigh unto them', proceeded to shower abuse on the apparitor. According to the archbishop they used 'unfitting, vile and spiteful words and demeanour'. What this phrase hides appears from the statements of Gold's witnesses, especially Peter Lee; Dodworth, too, deposed under oath. When the apparitor brought the citation into the church, Henry Kyng asked to see it. He studied it for a long time and then delivered himself of the opinion that 'it were well done to make the said apparitor to eat this citation', adding that 'it were a pity they lived if they did not cut off a leg or an arm of him or [before] that he departed from thence'. Dodworth protested that 'he was not to be blamed for he did but his lord's commandment', but Kyng only retorted ('making a fillip with his hand'), 'a turd for thy lord'. Now Stevyn took over, calling Dodworth a knave — one point that Dodworth himself would not swear to – and asserting that he would neither obey the citation nor accept service. According to Lee, Thomas Gold advised him to consult 'counsel learned in the spiritual law', but Stevyn rejected this reasonable if unseasonable advice. All this took place in the chancel, but after Kyng's contemptuous words George Wryght went further up, waving his sword and swearing to cut off some limb of the apparitor's. Throughout this time the vicar was saying mass in an adjoining chapel, this irreverent behaviour continuing from the gospel to the reception of the sacrament. Because the quarrel was attracting a crowd, Gold thought best to take Dodworth to his house. The witnesses disagreed as to his motives: one thought Gold feared for the apparitor's life, but others held he only wished to avoid 'inconvenience that was then like to have followed thereof', though that phrase could cover anything from an angry word to wholesale slaughter. Dodworth himself admitted that no one troubled them on the way to Gold's place, nor did he hear the altercation which others alleged occurred when the four Londoners followed Gold to his house. Henry Kyng, 'picking quarrels', charged Gold with calling the parishioners churls and beggars and said 'he was called Mr Gold but might well be called otherwise'. Gold protested his innocence of any name-calling, but Matthew Kyng swore by God's soul and by the mass that he had used words like churls, beggars and runaways,* laid his hand upon his sword and exclaimed that Gold 'had better to have meddled with his father than with him'.[38]

The evidence of Gold's party is clearcut and damning enough, even though the apparitor, whose alleged peril was the excuse for bringing the matter later before Star Chamber, proved the least eager witness. Since he was

* I.e. he had called the villagers serfs, a pretty bad insult.

also the only man not party to the internal troubles of Hayes, his moderation suggests some exaggeration in the rest. However, when the alleged rioters were asked what had happened they tended to confine themselves to general denials.[39] Henry Kyng remembered the apparitor citing Stevyn, but some eight months after the event he could not recall what words were then spoken. He could not say if Stevyn misbehaved as alleged, but then 'this deponent sayeth he understandeth no Latin'. One supposes he meant to deny that he was ever asked his opinion of the citation. As for himself, all he said to Dodworth was a gentle rebuke: 'Thou hast not done well to trouble all the parish at this time'. He only went to Gold's house later to appeal to the farmer to drop his suits against people in the parish, but when Gold retorted 'I have naught to do with you, but an [if] you will I will have to do with you,' he left him. Greenwood varied between not knowing what had been said and denying that other alleged words had been spoken. He added one point of value by stating that Stevyn appeared to his citation a few days later. It is one of the weak points in the archbishop's version that he does not mention what happened about the citation; now it would seem that the man cited did, in fact, make his appearance in court, though this does not mitigate the angry and violent scene of 6 June. Thomas Bradley, luckily for himself, went to morning mass that Whit-monday and was not present at Dodworth's intrusion. Stevyn himself blithely maintained that his only reason for asking Henry Kyng to look at the citation was that he wished to know the date on which he was to appear. From these depositions it seems that Nicholas Kyng was also cited; he said that the apparitor called his name just as the vicar was elevating the host which made him upbraid Dodworth with the words that 'he might have watched his time better'.

Thus the archbishop's first attempt to help Thomas Gold collect his tithe by citing at least two recalcitrant parishioners to appear before him somewhat misfired. The men cited were inhabitants of Hayes, but Hayes had that day visitors from London who would not let the apparitor get away with it. The scene was at the least very unpleasant and irreverent, even if the uglier possibilities of personal violence are exaggerated in the report. The defendants warmly denied the possession of weapons; what is clear is that they got extremely angry at Dodworth's appearance – which admittedly was badly timed, but apparitors had to choose a time when their victims were likely to be in a predictable place – and that they behaved in a most unseemly manner. The men cited may well have obeyed; we hear no more of the whole business and do not know what happened.

Before the archbishop again responded to his pressure, Thomas Gold exacerbated tempers further by suing out a writ of *replevin* against William Stevyn.* This was to be served on 26 June 1530 by Walter Hunt, the archbishop's bailiff who, as Gold correctly remarks, 'hath the return of all writs and the execution of them there'. That was by now all the meaning a franchise had: the carrying out of legal processes including the king's which could no longer be kept out (and *replevin*, like *non omittas* and *withernam*, was a royal writ) fell to the franchise-holder's officers, not to the sheriff of the county. Hunt attended matins at Hayes parish church and shortly before the procession asked Stevyn for a word. Stevyn turned upon

* The writ is explained above (footnote, p. 194). Stevyn had allegedly taken two 'counterpoints' (counterpanes ?) from Gold which he refused to return. The action used by Gold implies that Stevyn had done so to satisfy some alleged claim of his own; straight theft would have had other consequences.

him, called him a 'false harlot, false knave and bald knave', and accused him of having come to arrest him. Hunt said he had only a *replevin* to serve; would Stevyn allow him to come to his house and point out the goods which Gold was claiming? Stevyn retorted he would 'lay him upon the bald pate' if he came. Towards the end of the service Stevyn came to sit in the choir ('where he hath not used to do because he cannot sing'), together with Matthew Kyng, Henry Greenwood and George Wryght, those London friends who had stood by him when the citation was served. All four were armed, and Wryght had his naked sword lying before him. Shouting 'with clamorous and higher voices than the choir did sing', they told Hunt to be gone or they would so handle him 'that he never be able to serve any warrant'. Lee, vested in his alb and about to say mass, told them to be quiet or leave, whereupon Kyng seized him by the front of his clothes, put his hand on his dagger, and said in a fury: 'Wilt thou command us out of the chancel? We will not avoid [leave] for thee, for we have as good authority to be here as thou hast.' Thomas Gold called on Rowse to keep the peace, but the constable never stirred. Gold only succeeded in drawing Vincent's attention who threatened to pull him out and 'pluck his surplice over his ears'. Rowse then remarked, loudly enough to be heard by everybody: 'By the mass, these *replevins* will cause some man to be slain or harvest be done'; at which Gold, justifiably enough, warned him that such words were incendiary in the circumstances. The four rioters repeated their threats against Hunt and shook and slapped Gold on arms and shoulders; Lee declared himself convinced that if Gold had 'once moved or stirred against them' when thus illtreated he would have been killed.[40]

This was the story told by Gold's party, some of whom

added conviction by saying that they had not been present and knew only what they had been told. There was no attempt to pretend a general knowledge. The other side could not deny that something had taken place, but according to them it was all very peaceful.[41] Stevyn maintained that Hunt came during divine service to tell him of the *replevin*, to which Stevyn, thinking it was a warrant for his arrest, replied: 'I pray you, be content and make no business here, for my lord of Canterbury said that no bailiff should serve no writ within the church and churchyard.' Others joined in asserting it was a shame to arrest him at that time. One of them was Nicolls, also under the impression that an arrest was in the wind. However, unlike Stevyn who denied all the rest, he had heard Gold call on Rowse to keep the peace (why, if things were so quiet?) and Rowse's reply that he saw no one about to break it. Rowse himself made no mention of this exchange; he knew that Hunt wished to serve the *replevin* and had him to dinner after church when Hunt only told him that he had had ill words from young Kyng. Of all the rest of the story he professed himself ignorant, but he added that Gold came to him later to have him note that 'it was a *replevin* that he would have had the bailiff to have served' – not, one infers was his point, a warrant of arrest. Gold seems still to have been concerned not to be mistaken by the village. Bradley was away from Hayes and Henry Kyng overseas; but Greenwood spoiled things by telling a different story. He knew nothing of the misunderstanding about an intended arrest: as he told it, Hunt simply left Stevyn, saying he had done, when Stevyn denied possession of the disputed goods. He admitted that Lee told them to leave the chancel (though he denied all the noise and riotous behaviour) and gave Kyng's reply as 'we may sit here to serve God as well as ye'. Between them, the defendants really lead one to a confident belief in the essentials of Gold's accusations. It may well be that the degree of noise, the violence of the threats, and especially the presence of naked weapons were exaggerated, but it is hard to doubt that Stevyn and his friends resisted the service of a royal writ with some vigour, used improper language to the representative of the archbishop, and caused a very unseemly scene in church. The story that an arrest was suspected reads a little like an excuse invented after the event, though of course Stevyn – perhaps only too well aware that he stood in danger of apprehension – may genuinely have mistaken Hunt's intention. Even if he did, there is every reason to suppose from the evidence that he persisted in his behaviour after the matter had been explained.

But hard as it was to get the law served at Hayes, the authorities were not yet ready to give up, and soon after the failure of the *replevin* Warham took his turn again. Since the complaint was that divers parishioners would not lay out their corn as by custom they should, the archbishop sent an injunction to Henry Gold 'for reformation thereof', ordering the vicar to declare its tenor in the parish.[42] Gold read the injunction a first time in church on 24 July 1530 and stirred up another riot. A crowd led by Thomas Bradley and including William Rowse, Nicholas Kyng, John Nicolls, Nicholas Vincent, William Hill, George Osmond, William Bailly, John Aleyn, William Austen, Edmund Cope and Richard Hill* rushed up to the pew occupied by the vicar to protest against these archiepiscopal orders. Bradley struck the pew a violent blow with his fist and shouted: 'By God's soul, thou art but a wretch, and it is pity thou livest and that ever thou

---

* The pen reluctantly abandons the notion that the list should start with Bill Brewer.

wert vicar here.' This was followed by a general hubbub
– 'terrible exclamation', says Lee, many men 'speaking
and crying out together at one season'. It was not easy
afterwards to establish who had said what, though William
Hill could be identified as the man who threatened the
vicar with 'I would see who dare be so bold to declare any
such commandments here'. There were more positive
threats as well, variously reported as 'it were well done to
pluck him out of the church by the ears and to cast him
over the church walls' or 'draw him in pieces' or 'throw
him in the horsepool' or 'hurl him over the pale'. Once
again all this noise went on inside the church itself, just
after the gospel during the mass, for Gold had chosen that
moment to read the injuction. For the present, however,
noise was all that happened.

Either Gold and Warham exaggerated the riot –
though this, as we shall see, does not seem likely – or
the brothers Gold at least had plenty of courage. On the
following Sunday (31 July) Henry again rose after the
gospel to read the injunction a third time; it is not known
when he gave it its second proclamation, but presumably
he did so at some service in midweek when attendance
was thin and the troublemakers were absent. The third
reading was never to be completed. Gold had barely
started when much the same crowd as on the 24th took
up the challenge. Bradley and Vincent ran up to the vicar
and told him he was not to 'declare my lord's commandment here, for if thou doest we shall pluck thee and thy
brother both out of the church by the ears'. Was their
vocabulary really so limited, or should the sameness of
the threats make one wonder? The rest of the mob then
closed ranks round their leaders, and the vicar abandoned
the attempt. Nicolls was alleged to have shouted, 'it
were great shame for us to suffer these two wretches to

rule all us and to declare such commandments here' and to have sworn by God's soul that 'it were alms to make them to eat them'. At this point, while the crowd was milling round' the vicar's pew and working themselves into a noisy but, one feels, inactive temper, matters grew more serious with the women taking a hand. A mob of them gathered, including especially the wives of Nicholas Spurling, William Parke and John Power; interestingly enough the men and women rioters do not seem to have included any man-and-wife teams. At any rate, the witnesses told how the women, rolling or 'striking' up their sleeves, advanced into the church, shouting 'you men, get ye hence and let us wryght [put] harness on, and we shall pluck them out of the church and throw them over the church walls'; though here too the confusion was sufficient for some witnesses to substitute the horsepond for the churchyard walls and for others to deny hearing any threats of harness and killing.

Thus spurred on, the younger men turned after all to action. William Stevyn and Michael Harding yelled they were coming after the vicar; persuading two others (George Bennett and Richard Myng) to join them, they passed into the chancel only to be pushed back with somewhat surprising ease by Roger Chamley, Gold's servant, assisted by a certain Robert Webb. Now there occurred one of those bits of by-play which lend such verisimilitude to these semi-formalized descriptions in court. One of the men who sang in the choir was one Richard Woodgate. Myng and Bennett demanded his assistance and for a moment he hesitated. Then his wife was seen to push her way through the throng to appeal to him 'for the passion of God to avoid [leave] the chancel and not to meddle in any case'. Woodgate let off a string of oaths, 'with a great clap' slammed a book he was

holding on the pew in which he had (one supposes) half
risen, and 'in a great fury' went off with his wife. Angry
as apparently he was at this open surrender to petticoat
influence, he had probably done wisely. At least Thomas
Troughton was just then telling Lee near the high altar
that if the vicar were to read the injunction after all he
would be killed. Henry Gold seems to have thought so too,
for he now turned to William Rowse and charged him to
see the peace kept. Rowse took this the wrong way: he
commanded the vicar 'in the king's name' not to read the
archbishop's order, 'for if thou dost here will be man-
slaughter'. The vicar received a similar warning from Mr
Thomas Burbage who (described as a gentleman) seems
to have felt out of place and frightened by these riotous
proceedings on the part of his inferiors.[43] So far from
asserting himself he asked Gold to abandon the injunction
or 'there would be mischief and murder done'; he added
that he would wish the vicar to remember this warning
'for his discharge'. One man in Hayes at least was afraid
of the consequences.

It had in any case become clear to Gold that he could
not proceed with the injunction, and with his surrender
on this point the church emptied. But the anticlerical
party wished to make sure and to remind the brothers that
these doings would not be suffered any longer, and so
they staged a demonstration that same evening at evensong, coming in strength to church with their hands full
of cudgels and bills. 'Such manner in coming to the
church hath not been seen there before,' as the summary
of evidence remarks, and all the witnesses were interrogated on this point – as though the matter could have
been overlooked if it had been the custom of Hayes to
attend divine service armed to the teeth. The injunction
had to be dropped, 'to the great derogation and hurt', as

Warham complained, 'of the said archbishop's power and jurisdiction.'

This, of course, is the story as told by Gold's men. Bradley's version was very different.[44] He maintained that the first two readings of the injunction passed off without any disturbance; when Gold wished to read it a third time, Bradley politely requested him to wait 'until they of the parish know more of my lord of Canterbury's pleasure'. It is indeed likely that Gold's enemies distrusted his influence at Canterbury and wished to have a chance of putting their side before the archbishop. However, the vicar got very angry and swore that 'there should come down a great curse for them'. Bradley replied 'that it should be a wretched deed for him so to do', and the vicar's threat provoked a great outcry, though the deponent would not swear to specific words, saw no women involved, and did not think that anyone meditated physical violence against the vicar and the constable: when Gold asked for the peace to be kept Rowse replied, 'keep the peace yourself and no man here will meddle with you' – a comment which, despite the riotous behaviour of the other side, had much justice. Rowse himself told a very similar story: the general shout went up in response to Gold's threat of a curse on the village, and no specific words or speakers could be identified in the 'rumour and exclamation'. Unfortunately for the credit of the anti-Gold party, he produced yet a third version of his own words with the vicar; he may have felt that even those recorded by Bradley did not show him either sufficiently peaceful or sufficiently active about his duties. He said that when charged to keep the peace he remarked: 'I see no man here about to break the peace' – a really fine bit of eye-closing – and went on to those around, 'let us go out of the church and let them chide alone'. On his showing

Rowse was a splendid example of the Dogberry breed; on
that of Thomas Gold, however, he was sinister rather than
ineffectual. The other defendants took up much the same
position: the trouble was caused by the vicar's threat and
there was never any danger of murder or manslaughter.
Nicholas Kyng, absent on the 24th 'at a bridal' at Staines
but present on the 31st, produced yet another version of
Rowse's reply to Gold: 'I charge thee keep thou the peace,
for I see no man so like to break the peace as thou art'.

The mere accumulation of more convincing detail,
which Gold's witnesses certainly produced, is not by itself
perfect proof of their truth, nor is their general agreement
on this detail since all the depositions were taken a year
or more after the event and a good deal of comparing and
concerting had clearly been done. But apart from the
story of the citation in which the archbishop's charges
were seen to be nearer the truth than the villagers' replies,
two things tell against Bradley and his men in this matter
of the injunction. One is the fact that the witnesses against
him included one man, Edward Cope, who on the 24th
had been among the mob that followed him. Cope maintained that Bradley had played on the fears of himself 'and
other ignorant persons' by alleging that the vicar 'had
gotten a curse like unto the curse which the vicar some
time had gotten at Northwood, that is that they should be
accursed with bell, book and candle; after which curse so
denounced, the parishioners at Northwood caused the
vicar to turn the curse to the brambles that grew in a
field there, and so he did, and so from that day hither
(they said) there grew no brambles in that field, which if
the said vicar of Hayes had done this deponent judged it
not to be well done'. Bradley, then, had got up a mob
against Gold on the occasion of the first (not, as he said,
the third) reading by playing on local superstitions and

by making out that an injunction which ordered the proper payment of tithe was a solemn curse and excommunication. Cope's change of side can only have resulted from his discovery that he had been duped; if Bradley's version were the true one, Cope would only have been confirmed in his fears by the vicar's promise of a curse and would not have turned witness for the prosecution.

The other thing that told rather heavily against Bradley on this occasion was the evidence of premeditation that could be produced by Peter Lee and others. Lee said he knew that there would be trouble because on the night of 30 July a certain Richard Pope came secretly to him to warn him of a conspiracy being hatched at Rowse's house. According to Pope, a group gathered there had decided to kill the vicar if he read the injunction again on the following day; much too afraid to be seen talking to Gold in person, he begged Lee to pass the warning on. At about the same time Agnes Gold received word from London that Henry Kyng, Bradley and others were plotting to kill her husband. The message came from Mrs Daws who had the information from one of her maids whose sister (Joan Bynfeld) was servant to Henry Kyng. Greatly perturbed by this message, Mrs Gold persuaded the curate to write in haste to the Middle Temple in order to warn Gold. However, it seems that this story at least was not true, or rather that Agnes and Lee had been misled. The villagers were later able to point out that Joan admitted in the Star Chamber that she had made it all up: she had never heard Henry Kyng threaten any such plots, but Thomas Gold had before that promised her a year's wages if she would testify against the inhabitants of Hayes.[45] Still, this does not prove Lee a liar, though it throws a useful light on Thomas Gold, nor does it altogether disprove that Bradley and the

rest were near to violence. In order to drive home the
standing danger to the brothers, one of Gold's witnesses
accused Stevyn of saying he would thrust his dagger into
the rector whenever he met him, even if it were before
the altar; another remembered Vincent boasting repeatedly 'that if he took either the vicar or Gold handsomely,
he would make them that they should not claw it off as
long as they lived'. It must be beyond serious doubt that
the tale told by the archbishop and supported by Gold's
witnesses was nearer the truth. Two attempts to exercise
ecclesiastical jurisdiction at Hayes had only led to riots,
and on the second occasion at least the situation had been
very ugly. In assessing its ugliness, however, it is worth
remembering that so far no one except Dixon seems to
have suffered so much as a box on the ear.

Warham, at any rate, was persuaded of the justice of
Gold's complaints, and having failed to secure him his
tithe he now at least attempted to discipline the parish.
On 18 September 1530 he sent a precept to the vicar to
cite the churchwardens (Nicholas Vincent and Roger
Stanys) as well as some others ('called sidesmen') before
his commissary at Newington at the visitation to be held
there. Gold told Lee to see the precept carried out. In
the excited state of the village this further persecution,
as it must have seemed to them, naturally touched off
another outburst. The churchwardens called on the
vicar after evensong and demanded to have the precept
which, they said, should have been sent to them directly;
no doubt Gold would not give it because he suspected
that the document would never be seen again. The
churchwardens also declared roundly that none of the men
cited would appear. As they were leaving in a fury, Vincent could not restrain himself from saying that 'two
such polled priests and knave priests should not order nor

rule them'. When he had got into the churchyard he added
that he would so 'bait' the two brothers and their friends
that all the knaves they had 'should not dare to be out of
their doors'. These exchanges had also taken place in
church, but Lee's testimony makes it plain that at least
the churchwardens had waited until the service was over.
Warham complained both of the 'spiteful and opprobrious
words and misdemeanours' used and of the fact that he
could not enforce his precepts. He was soon to find that
Bradley and his friends would not confine their opprobrious demeanour to disobedience; they were about to
attack.[46]

On 16 October 1530, after previously concerting their
plans, Bradley, Rowse and their leading supporters way-
laid Thomas, Henry and Agnes Gold on their way to
church and asked to speak with them. The Golds stopped;
Bradley told them that Lee had been dismissed and should
no longer serve the parish church; the Golds went on,
disconcerted and to the accompaniment of derisive
laughter ('hayght, hayght, hayght!') from Nicolls. In thus
discharging the curate, without the knowledge or consent of the archbishop and contrary to the vicar's wishes,
they had – as Warham urged – usurped the archbishop's
authority. It is not easy to see what they thought they
were about. Presumably they felt goaded into action by
the constant writs and process called down upon them by
the obnoxious vicar and his worse lawyer brother; one
can only suppose that, realizing that they could touch
neither of the Golds, they decided to strike at Henry
Gold's creature, Peter Lee. The vicar was a pluralist; he
occasionally took the service at Hayes but more commonly
(it would appear) left it to Lee; thus if Lee were to go he
would be in something of a pickle. When interrogated
later, Bradley and Rowse denied that they had dismissed

the priest: they had asked Henry Gold to do so. Bradley, however, admitted the village's determination that Lee 'should sing no more there with any gear belonging to the parish' until the archbishop's pleasure be known. This obscure rider probably refers to a matter alluded to with similar obscurity by John Nicolls who deposed that Lee had quarrelled with another priest and that the archbishop had ordered both to be put out of their offices. By their decision about Lee the parish claimed to have obeyed, while the vicar had resisted. Since Warham described the villagers' action as usurpation of his authority – even though it is no doubt true that his complaint rested upon Thomas Gold's report – this sanctimonious pretence had little to rest on.[47]

The fact was that, however they cared to put it, Bradley and his friends had determined to be rid of Lee. Since Henry Gold would not give way they could not prevent Lee from staying at the vicarage and appearing in church; they therefore resolved to make it impossible for him to say mass or conduct any services. On the evening of the 16th they called the parish clerk and told him not to let Lee have any vestments, chalices or ornaments. On the 24th, a Monday, Henry Gold asked for this 'gear' and, thinking that Gold himself would say mass, Troughton let him have it. But the vicar told Lee to say mass, and when the churchwardens discovered this they abused Troughton for acting contrary to the parish's orders. Though they calmed down after a while, they went to the church about noon that day and took away the vestments and the rest. They did not keep them long, only till All Souls' Day (2 November); but their action, by which for the first time they quite definitely overstepped the mark, caused enough trouble as it was. Poor Margaret Andrew was churched on the 26th

without benefit of mass. No mass was said on the feast of
SS. Simon and Jude (28 October) or on the Sunday after
(the 30th), though on both occasions Lee stood up in the
church and offered to do his part if the ornaments were
returned to him. The only reaction came from William
Hill who in a loud voice charged Thomas Troughton to
withhold the things and declared himself ready to 'bear
and abide the peril and jeopardy that should fall thereupon'. Lee said that Hill and Bradley took the congrega-
tion to hear mass elsewhere, but this is not confirmed by
anyone else, and since it is for once a point which Lee –
the constant eye-witness – would be in no position to
avouch at first hand, it must remain in doubt whether
the ringleaders were sufficiently careful of the parish's
spiritual welfare. Another attempt to recover the ornaments was made on All Hallows (1 November) when
Thomas Gold himself appealed for their return since it
was a principal feast. On this occasion the leaders –
Bradley, Rowse, Vincent, Nicholas Kyng, Osmond and
William Hill – were away, so that Gold may have thought
his chances better. However, the younger generation were
quite ready to hold the fort. Stevyn, as usual, took the
lead, swearing loudly and affirming that he would pull
Lee from the high altar 'and so out of the church by the
ears' rather than that he should say mass. He was supported by some of whom we have hitherto heard almost
nothing – George Flee, Roger Hill, William Hale and
William Austen – with Hale remarking: 'Now our heads
be absent and gone, we poor fellows will rule these matters
by strong hand'. Such threats begin to take one into the
dark and dangerous realm of social unrest. Lee described
the deplorable situation during those days: he was forced
to say the services in his plain gown, and when he
sprinkled holy water some of the parish spat at it in their

spite. Stevyn, leaning against the choir door, remarked that he would 'liefer hear mass in a sheep-cote' than hear Lee's mass. The village refused to let Thomas Gold have the surplice he usually wore at service 'and so he was fain to take a child's surplice, called a rochet, to serve God with'.

The testimony of the accused does little to alter the impression derived from these reports. They admitted telling the clerk not to let Lee have the ornaments, even though they did not explicitly admit taking them away themselves. Nicolls maintained that when Thomas Gold enquired whether mass was not to be said on All Saints' Day he replied piously, 'God forbid else, and tomorrow too'; but though they would, he said, have let the vicar have the ornaments for such high feasts, he had already borrowed some elsewhere. This seems improbable, but it is likely that the possibility was mentioned and made them restore the vestments and chalices on the 2nd. Another equally powerful factor in their surrender may lie in the reason for the absence of Bradley and the other leaders on the morning of the 1st: it emerges from their depositions that they were up before the archbishop that day. Of this Warham says nothing in his charge, a point which may incline us more favourably to the villagers' complaint that they were constantly being harried and troubled by the law, especially the law of the church. Full as our information is, we do not know the whole story; it would be well to remember that. Stevyn denied the various words attributed to him, and so the tale of improbable innocence continued.

As far as one can judge at this distance, there can be no doubt that the parish had really gone too far and that Warham and Gold now felt the time for energetic measures upon them. After a year of troubles, some of which they had certainly brought on themselves, they resorted to the authority of the king's Council. At some time unknown, but certainly before the end of 1530, both Warham and Gold put in bills in Star Chamber. The archbishop cast his complaint in the form of articles 'exhibited unto the king's highness and his most honourable Council' against 'divers misruled and evil-disposed persons' at Hayes, for their offences 'as well contrary to the laws of Holy Church as also contrary to the king's peace, his laws and dignity, to the great hurt and parlous example of all good and true Christian people'. He listed four points affecting him: the citation, the injunction, the precept to the churchwardens, and the usurpation of his authority; he complained that 'no precept, commandment nor citation . . . for causes spiritual' could be served or enforced at Hayes, with the result that the service of God and the devotions of Christian people were increasingly suffering; and he asked for a remedy in Star Chamber.[48] To this complaint – which, allowing for some slight partisan exaggeration, seems justified enough – the defendants could only reply that this charge was just one more stage in the vexatious proceedings with which Archdeacon Warham had troubled them before and deny all riotous behaviour; Warham's replication succeeded in eliminating the red herring of his relative's long-dead proceedings.[49] At about the same time Gold presented his charges, cast in the same form; the terms in which especially the heading and the conclusion of his bill are expressed make it plain that he and Warham acted in concert or (more probably) that he had prepared both documents. He also mentioned the citation, injunction and precept, but he concentrated on the matters which particularly concerned him: the *non omittas*, *replevin*, Bradley's misdemeanours (in organizing the strike over

213

tithe), the escape of Page, the misrule in Rowse's house (the various charges of gambling and unlawful games). His bill, too, pointed out the impossibility of serving a writ in Hayes and prayed for redress. The defendants' answer repeated, almost word for word, that which they had made to Warham's bill.[50]

At any time the Council in Star Chamber would have taken up such charges. The defiance of the villagers put the enforcement of the law, their particular care, into jeopardy, and the riotous doings alleged brought matters easily within their competence. One of the accusers, at least, was a great man of the realm – not, indeed, a member of the active Council (his age and Wolsey's long cold-shouldering saw to that) but still, as he reminded them, primate of England. The moment, moreover, was not propitious for the men of Hayes. Wolsey's fall in October 1529 for a time paradoxically revived rather than weakened the powers of orthodoxy and clerical ascendancy. The lord chancellor of the moment, by virtue of his office president of the Star Chamber, was no longer that splendid prelate one of whose chief preoccupations had been the humbling of his brother of Canterbury, but that devout layman, Sir Thomas More, who was doing his best to assist the bishops in their renewed campaign against heresy. In 1531 little Thomas Bilney, proto-martyr of the English Reformation, was to die at the stake, and other heresy trials were even then proceeding. The years 1530–32 were in some ways a bad time for a quarrel with the Church: they saw the last struggles of the old order to rebuild the defences against dangerous innovations which the king's quarrel with the pope was encouraging despite Henry VIII's own predilections.[51] London was notoriously a centre of anticlerical disaffection, and here was a case in which some citizens had helped villagers not far away in their defiance of the ecclesiastical authorities. The villagers were in trouble.

Matters proceeded through the interrogatories and depositions which have supplied the bulk of the material used in this reconstruction, and even as we have been forced to see that the parish had certainly committed serious offences so must the court have done. The case was investigated in a somewhat peculiar sequence. The defendants were interrogated early, between December 1530 and January 1531; but it was not until August 1531 that the court got round to taking depositions to the same interrogatories from Gold's witnesses, and the last of these was not heard until October. At some point the defendants were committed to ward, and these dates suggest that the court wished to secure their persons at once in order to take their statements first. There is about these proceedings a definite air of hostility to the villagers. The prison in which they found themselves was almost certainly the Fleet. Not only was this the prison which the Star Chamber habitually used for the safe-keeping of men accused before it whom it was desired either to prevent from running away or to treat harshly because they were thought guilty; in addition, the paper from which we know of their confinement speaks of 'the warden', an officer specifically associated with the Fleet prison.

This paper is an appeal from the inhabitants to someone unnamed, rather roughly written as though it were the work of the appellants rather than some lawyer. The addressee is called 'your mastership', and the temptation is great to identify him with that one man whom the records of the day most commonly call by that title.[52] But if the villagers tried to enlist the services of Thomas Cromwell (not then a member of the inner Council but in the king's employ), the point cannot be proved, nor can it be shown that they got anywhere with him. They used their appeal to explain the terms of tithe at Hayes, to deny the charges of gaming and unruly behaviour, to point out that the accusation of conspiring against Gold's life had fallen down in court, and to recall their happy relations with Henry Gold's predecessor. In addition they attempted to discredit Gold's witnesses. They would gladly see his mastership and explain in more detail, but the warden would not let them go unless they gave sureties 'to be true prisoner' at a cost which they could not afford. The fact that the warden could offer that much is proof that they were in custody only pending trial.

And this is where the story breaks off. We do not know what the court decided or what punishments, if any, were inflicted. The evidence, as has been said, supports Gold and the archbishop. It is as certain as can be that repeated attempts to use the law against these villagers were defeated by them, to the accompaniment of much rudeness and some violence. It is certain that they tried to evade their duty to pay tithe and that on several occasions they behaved most improperly in church. It is clear that their feelings for their clergy varied from contempt to hatred, and this must include Archdeacon Warham so that Thomas Gold being a lay farmer does not affect the issue. Their 'anticlericalism' had little to do with religion: they certainly were no heretics but attended mass regularly and with formal devotion. At the same time, their doings over Lee's dismissal came very near to the complete flouting of all ecclesiastical authority and even, since they removed the mass-gear from the church, to sacrilege. Clearly this did not bother them greatly: they were concerned to win their battle with the brothers Gold. In that battle the brothers had the legal rights; of this there can be no doubt. But the villagers had a case, too. The farmer and his clerical brother behaved with arrogance and some degree, at least, of greed. They quarrelled readily and sought to get all they could out of the village. Bradley and his followers had no right to withhold the tithe from Gold, but in another sense what right had Gold to the tithe? The fact is that this payment, intended to support the spiritual cure of souls of those who rendered it, had long become no more than a straight rent from land. All the evils of secularization, so often ascribed to the effects of the Reformation, were fully present, and though the Church of England was to fight on for centuries both to justify and to collect the tithe it cannot be denied, and should not be ignored, that the parish of Hayes regarded such payments as a deep grievance as early as 1529.* Indeed, the only positive way in which this case differs from the later struggles of the Church to maintain its revenues lies in the probability that the villagers had the worst of it in Star Chamber. That, however, is nothing to do with Rome and Reformation but was due to the vigour of the Council in enforcing the law and the special circumstances of 1530 and 1531.

One would not use a single instance to prove any general assertion, but one may justifiably point to a case in which much detail is known in order to test generalizations. In this respect this story of the war which Hayes in Middlesex waged against rector, vicar, curate and archbishop throws the light of positive understanding on that famous anticlericalism of early Tudor England,

* The point has to be made because as recently as 1956 it could be argued that the Reformation made a significant difference in the story. In view of Thomas Gold's doings it is amusing to see Mr Hill maintain (*Economic Problems*, 90) that before the Reformation the confessional rather than the courts were used to enforce tithe. Cf. also his constant use of the Reformation as a watershed in the Church's economic affairs, esp. in his *Conclusion*.

and grave doubt on attempts to ascribe the difficulties and insufficiencies of the Elizabethan Church, whether economic or spiritual, to the Reformation.

Though unfortunately we have to leave Bradley, Rowse and the rest in the Fleet, awaiting with but little hope the verdict of Star Chamber, we ought not to conclude without what is in some ways the true end of the story. A worse fate was round the corner for Thomas and Henry Gold than any they could contrive for their adversaries at Hayes. Henry, that harmless and ordinary careerist, involved himself in no less a cause than that of Elizabeth Barton, the so-called Nun of Kent. This unhappy woman, a servant girl who for years had been gaining a reputation for sanctity by trances and prophecies, in 1533 took it into her head to prophesy dire things for the king unless he put away Anne Boleyn and restored matters to where they had been in politics and religion before these late upheavals had got under way. Stage-managed carefully by some interested ecclesiastics, the Nun scored a brief success, though later she was constrained to confess that her alleged visions had been pretended. Why Henry Gold should have fallen for her we cannot say; any form of enthusiasm seems out of place in his character and career, as far as they have been displayed before us. Perhaps the death of his patron, Warham, in August 1532 proved a serious setback and a turning point in his life; perhaps he was simply and truly attached to the old ways in religion.[53] In any case, he was in good company: Bishop Fisher of Rochester regarded the Nun as a saint, and Sir Thomas More considered her worthy of respect though he changed his mind after looking into her claims.[54] Poor Henry Gold did not withdraw. The government struck hard, and the act of attainder which in February 1534 condemned Elizabeth Barton to death also included the

names of Henry and Thomas Gold.[55] Henry, attainted
of high treason, was to suffer death; Thomas, guilty of the
lesser offence of misprision of treason, was to be imprisoned at the king's pleasure and lose all his property. Before
he mounted the scaffold on 20 April 1534,[56] Henry wrote
a letter to Cromwell in which he asked that his brother
might be pardoned; he reveals here a much more attractive character than his doings at Hayes ever suggested.[57]
Making no further appeal for himself, he asked Cromwell
'to have compassion and pity of my poor brother, for of
truth he was miserably deceived by that false dissembling
Nun'. Thomas had only committed the crime of trusting
to his own brother and to some virtuous monks of
Richmond who in their turn had been deceived. 'His
living, as your mastership doth know, lieth most by his
credence, the which taken away, he, his wife and his children be in manner but undone. Wherefore, for Christ's
passion, have compassion of him and his. . . .'

However mercifully Cromwell might feel inclined –
and it is noticeable that Gold with every appearance of
sincerity assumed this quality in him – he could hardly at
this point rescue one of the people who had put Henry
VIII in a great stew by encouraging prophecies concerning his early demise. How much Thomas Gold lost through
his misfortunes is not known; certainly late in 1533,
before even the act of attainder clinched matters, Cranmer
(Warham's successor at Canterbury) was writing to
recommend a man to Archdeacon Warham for the farm of
Hayes which was vacant or was shortly to be so.[58] That he
lost Hayes, anyway, and suffered other troubles appears
from a letter which Christopher Ashton, servant to the
king, wrote to Cromwell in May 1535.[59] He had had
business with one Thomas Gold who, forgetting all caution, had begun to rail against the king and Cromwell.

He called Cromwell a false and bawdy wretch and a tyrant who had undone him and 'had put him from a parsonage that was worth £100 by the year'. According to Gold, Cromwell had tried to obtain the farm of Hayes for a friend of his (John Croke of the Chancery),[60] and when Gold had refused Cromwell saw to it that he spent an extra three months in the Tower. Ashton, full of virtue, offered to arrest this traitorous blasphemer, though he admitted that there was no other witness to the outburst. What truth there may have been in Gold's bitter grievances cannot appear. He seems to have forgotten his involvement with the Nun which was really responsible for all his losses, and it is not in the least clear why Cromwell should have bothered to solicit a man for a favour who had no longer got it to grant. That Gold might easily contract a permanent grudge against Cromwell, whom he would blame for his misfortunes, is quite another matter. However, what is really interesting is the outcome. If even half the ill laid to Cromwell's charge were true one would expect evidence of investigation – perhaps of stringent action – against one who had so abused him and spoken against the king. The only remaining notice, however, of Thomas Gold occurs on 26 August 1536: it grants him a general pardon for all past offences.[61]

A NOTE ON SOURCES

Manuscript sources, unless otherwise stated, are all to be found at the Public Record Office, London. I have quoted the records by a significant description rather than by the call number there in use, because this way they mean something to the reader; also, the P.R.O. prefer one to do so. For the convenience of researchers I may mention here that the three bodies of records most quoted in the book are Star Chamber Proceedings, Henry VIII (St. Ch. 2), State Papers of Henry VIII (S.P. 1), and Exchequer, King's Remembrancer, Memoranda Rolls (E. 159). Among printed sources, the most important has, of course, been *Letters and Papers, Foreign and Domestic, of the reign of Henry VIII* (ed. Brewer, Gairdner and Brodie, 1862–1929) which is quoted as *L.P.*, with a reference to the volume and number of the document calendared. Other abbreviations used to unburden the footnotes are *Cal. Pat.* for *Calendars of Patent Rolls* and *D.N.B.* for *Dictionary of National Biography*.

NOTES

I. FOOL OF OXFORD

1. R. B. Merriman, *Life and Letters of Thomas Cromwell* (1902), i. 118.

2. J. Foster, *Alumni Oxonienses 1500–1714*, iii. 1147.

3. *Athenae Oxonienses* (ed. Bliss), i. 147.

4. Conyers Read, *Bibliography of British History: Tudor Period*, no. 1102.

5. In his letter to Cromwell which is one of the chief sources of the story here put together: State Papers, Henry VIII, vol. 115, fo. 110v.

6. I have used the edition of 1827 (ed. R. J. Greening) as being the most accessible, though I have checked with editions of the sixteenth century.

7. State Papers, Henry VIII, vol. 115, fos. 95 seqq., part of a letter to Cromwell.

8. State Papers, Henry VIII, vol. 115, fos. 97–102.

9. For this see *Eynsham Cartulary* (ed. H. E. Salter, 1907), vol. i, p. xxxi. He was called Dunstone until his elevation to the episcopate.

10. *Victoria County History, Oxfordshire*, ii. 93; *L.P.* xii. II. 1120, 1246.

11. State Papers, Henry VIII, vol. 114, fo. 102 (*L.P.* xiii. I. 79[1]).

12. Star Chamber Proceedings, Henry VIII, bundle 34, file 11, docs. 4–7. The correct chronological sequence of these undated letters is 7, 6, 5, 4.

13. State Papers, Henry VIII, vol. 114, fos. 104–5.

14. Star Chamber Proc., Henry VIII, bundle 34, file 11, doc. 1.

15. I.e. a commission specially appointed for the purpose and empowered to try treason or felony.

16. *L.P.* xi. 1217 (20); Harcourt is there called William, but

222

this is certainly an error either of the calendar or of the chancery clerk who copied the commission on to the roll.

17. Fleurs and Banester occur frequently in the record; for Pye see *L.P.* xii. II. 1220.

18. *L.P.* xiii. I. 333, 359.

19. *L.P.* xii. I. 638; II. 967 (10).

20. *L.P.* xii. II. 952-3.

21. *L.P.* xiii. I. 1066.

22. Star Chamber Proc., Henry VIII, bundle 34, file 11, doc. 2.

23. State Papers, Henry VIII, vol. 115, fos. 107–12. The letter was written at least a little later; it is endorsed as being from 'John Parkins, banished Oxford for accusing the abbots of Eynsham and Osney of matters against the king'.

24. State Papers, Henry VIII, vol. 114, fos. 257–8.

25. Star Chamber Proc., Henry VIII, bundle 34, file 11, doc. 9.

26. Ibid. doc. 5; see above, pp. 32 f.

27. Ibid. doc. 3.

28. Ibid. doc. 8.

29. *L.P.* xii. I. 211.

30. Ibid. 261 (State Papers, Henry VIII, vol. 115, fo. 95).

31. *L.P.* xii. I. 261(2).

32. State Papers, Henry VIII, vol. 115, fo. 104.

33. Ibid. f. 105.

34. Ibid. fo. 113.

35. Ibid. fo. 115.

36. Ibid. fos. 116–17.

37. Ibid. fos. 118–19.

2. CAMBRIDGE RIOTS

1. Cambridge University Library, MS. Baker 26, p. 84.

2. The award is printed in full in C. H. Cooper, *Annals of Cambridge* (1842), i. 260 ff. It is worth reading for a better understanding of the sort of problems at issue.

3. Star Chamber Proc., Henry VIII, vol. 8, fo. 68. That John Chapman was a miller appears from John Lamb, *Documents*

Illustrative of the History of the University of Cambridge 1500–1572 (London, 1838), p. 40.

4. Star Chamber Proc., Henry VIII, vol. 8, fo. 70. The Chapmans were a leading burgess family; Hugh Chapman was mayor in 1514 (ibid. bundle 28, file 11).

5. Ibid. vol. 8, fos. 71–2.

6. Ibid. bundle 18, file 131.

7. Cooper, *Annals*, i. 353.

8. Star Chamber Proc., Henry VIII, vol. 8, fo. 69.

9. MS. Baker 26, p. 83.

10. Star Chamber Proc., Henry VIII, vol. 8, fos. 51–65.

11. MS. Baker 26, p. 83.

12. The following account is based on the university's bill (Star Chamber Proc. Henry VIII, vol. 8, fo. 69) and Mere's diary (MS. Baker 26, pp. 83–4).

13. The Friday in 'cleansing week', i.e. the Friday before Good Friday.

14. Star Chamber Proc. Henry VIII, bundle 22, file 360. Parker is included in J. A. Venn, *Alumni Cantabrigienses* and was therefore a member of the university; the rest may have been servants.

15. Star Chamber Proc., Henry VIII, bundle 25, file 131, doc. 1.

16. There were a first and a second draft of these interrogatories: ibid. vol. 8, fos. 55 and 51–4.

17. Ibid. fo. 57.

18. MS. Baker 26, p. 85.

19. Star Chamber Proc., Henry VIII, vol. 8, fo. 56.

20. Ibid. fos. 58–65.

21. Cf. *Tudor Proclamations in Facsimile*, publ. Society of Antiquaries (1897), [no. 12].

22. 23 Henry VIII, c. 3 (*Statutes of the Realm*, iii. 420).

23. E.g. in Ridley's and Wilkes's answers in this case, or in the university's answers to the town's articles concerning Stourbridge Fair (Lamb, op. cit., pp. 28 ff., esp. p. 29).

24. 25 Henry VIII, c. 1 (*Statutes of the Realm*, iii. 436 ff.).

25. All these details on Richard Lichfield are derived from a bill put in against him by the town (Star Chamber Proc., Henry VIII, bundle 28, file 11).

26. Star Chamber Proc., Henry VIII, bundle 26, file 178.

27. Ridley was in general a troublemaker. In May 1534 Chapman sent a man accused of treason to Thomas Cromwell with a letter in which he reported John Ridley as threatening the town authorities for putting the accused in prison (*L.P.* vii. 629).

28. *Grace Book Γ*, p. 288.

29. Ibid. pp. 289 f.

30. Star Chamber Proc., Henry VIII, 8, fo. 51: 'Interrogatories upon certain Instructions made by the king's attorney to the lord chancellor of England and other the lords of the king his most honourable Council, concerning certain misdemeanours and other unlawful assemblies committed and made within the town of Cambridge. . . .'

31. For this and the following documents cf. above, p. 63.

32. Merriman, *Life and Letters of Thomas Cromwell*, letters 106, 116, 124, 129.

33. Ibid. letters 186, 206.

3. INFORMING FOR PROFIT

1. Cf. G. D. Ramsay, 'The Smugglers' Trade', *English Overseas Trade in the Centuries of Emergence* (1957), ch. VI.

2. N. S. B. Gras, 'Tudor "Books of Rates" ', *Quarterly Journal of Economics*, xxvi (1912), pp. 766 ff.

3. *L.P.* xi. 1433.

4. Cf. A. P. Newton, 'The Establishment of the Great Farm of the English Customs', *Trans. R. Hist. Soc.*, 1918, pp. 129 ff.

5. Cf. also M. W. Beresford, 'The Common Informer, the Penal Statutes and Economic Regulation', *Economic History Review*, 2nd Ser., vol. x (1957), 221 ff. Much detail on informing activities under Elizabeth and later may be gathered from M. G. Davies, *The Enforcement of English Apprenticeship* (Harvard, 1956), esp. ch. II.

6. This part of the story is pieced together from three letters: Cromwell to the mayor of Southampton on 4 Sept. (Merriman, *Life and Letters of Thomas Cromwell*, 1902, i. 387), the mayor to Cromwell on 18 Oct. (*L.P.* vii. 1278), and Richard Lister to Cromwell on 8 Dec. (State Papers, Henry VIII, vol. 139, fo. 208). They raise difficult problems of dating. As *L.P. Add.* p. 353 n. points out, Lister's letter, being dated 'Wednesday Our Lady Day', determines the year – 1535 (not 1534, as *L.P.* vii. 1132, 1278 and Merriman assume). But if the date of 8 Sept. 1535, assigned to Lister's letter, be correct, we should have to suppose that Whelplay made his first catch at Southampton almost before he had time to get there. According to Lister, he left Southampton on the 7th, after business extending certainly over two and almost certainly over more days; yet Cromwell did not write him his letter of support till the 4th. I have therefore taken it that 'Our Lady Day' here means not the Nativity but the Conception (8 Dec.) which also fell on a Wednesday in 1535.

7. Exch. K.R. Mem. Rolls, 317, Easter, m. 7.

8. The act of 21 Henry VIII, c. 13, the so-called Pluralities Act, also forbade the clergy to engage in trade.

9. Star Chamber Proc., Henry VIII, bundle 20, file 126; bundle·17, file 107.

10. Ibid. bundle 17, file 117.

11. Walsh died about June–July 1542 (*L.P.* xvii. 499). According to the jury Whelplay had put his information into the Exchequer in 32 Henry VIII (1540–1): it looks as though he may have succeeded in obtaining a trial within two years.

12. Exch. K.R. Mem. Rolls, 317, Easter, m. 8d.

13. Ibid. 318, Michaelmas, m. 8d.

14. Ibid. Hillary, m. 17d.

15. Ibid. 319, Easter, m. 27.

16. Ibid. m. 32.

17. Ibid. Hillary, m. 4.

18. Ibid. m. 15. Peppys' will was proved in February 1542 (W. C. Pepys, *Genealogy of the Pepys Family*, 1952, p. 35).

19. Exch. K. R. Mem. Rolls, 317, Easter mm. 6, 7;

Trinity, mm. 10, 30; Michaelmas, mm. 17d, 25, 27; 319, Trinity, m. 9.

20. Ibid. 319, Hillary, mm. 15–22d.

21. Ibid. 320, Easter, m. 25.

22. State Papers Henry VIII, 243, fos. 169–70 (*L.P. Add.* 1490 [3]). The date is conjectural. Whelplay's references to his relations with the duke of Norfolk seem to me to put this paper before the duke's letter of 16 October 1540. Parts of the document suggest that it may well have been the complaint referred to as received from Whelplay in the Council minute of 9 Oct. 1540 (*L.P.* xvi. 137), or that at the very least it belonged to the same stage in Whelplay's affairs.

23. *L.P.* xvi. 137.

24. Ibid. 146–7. The other ministers approached were the lord chancellor, the chancellors of Augmentations and First Fruits, the general surveyors, and the master of Wards.

25. Ibid. 169, printed in full in *State Papers of Henry VIII* (1830–52), i. 650 ff.

26. *L.P.* xvi. 180.

27. Ibid. 180, 241.

28. State Papers, Henry VIII, 243, fos. 166–70 (two nearly identical copies). See *L.P. Add.* 1490 (1–2). The date may have been around 1540 because Whelplay referred to a certain Haynes who thirty-five years earlier had been 'officer of the silk-beam'. The only Haynes I have been able to find who might conceivably be the man is a certain Alexander, a citizen and woolman of London, who received a pardon on 16 February 1506 (*Cal. Pat. Henry VII*, ii. 446). The import of manufactured silk, with which the complaint is concerned, was prohibited in an act of 1504 (19 Henry VII, *c.* 21), and reformers of administrative details commonly looked for the last good order in the later years of Henry VII; both these points make a date thirty-five years after *c.* 1505 likely.

29. Workers in 'short silk' got 6*d.* a pound for winding, 10*d.* a pound for dyeing, and 6*d.* or more a pound for 'working of the bobbins'.

30. *L.P.* xx. ii. 788.

31. 31 Henry VIII, c. 8, the famous Act of Proclamations.

32. Star Chamber Proc., Henry VIII, bundle 28, files 14 and 24 ; bundle 29, files 96 and 175.

33. The proclamation does not survive, but its purport and date appear from Whelplay's bills and from a proclamation of May 1541 which lifted the ban as far as Calais was concerned (*L.P.* xvi. 844).

34. Star Chamber Proc., Henry VIII, bundle 27, files 40, 63, 64, 80, 87, 90 [and ibid. bundle 25, file 240], 91, 93 (twelve cases), 118.

35. Ibid. bundle 18, file 149.

36. Star Chamber Proc., Henry VIII, bundle 25, file 240.

37. Ibid. file 87.

38. Ibid. file 80.

39. Star Chamber Proc., Henry VIII, bundle 27, file 118. For Reneger cf. G. Connell-Smith, *Forerunners of Drake* (1954), esp. p. 137 where this incident is also referred to. I have no doubt that the informer spoke the truth.

40. Ibid. bundle 25, file 63.

41. The evidence for this episode consists of three interrogatories with answers, administered by Star Chamber (ibid. bundle 34, file 2).

42. Exch. K.R. Mem. Rolls, 317, Trinity, m. 10.

43. Star Chamber Proc., Henry VIII, bundle 27, file 125 (1).

44. The full Exchequer record is in K.R. Mem. Rolls, 317, Trinity, mm. 10, 10d, 28d.

45. Ibid. Michaelmas, m. 25.

46. Star Chamber Proc., Henry VIII, bundle 27, file 94.

47. Or the 1st, according to the bill in Star Chamber.

48. £100, by the time Whelplay approached Star Chamber.

49. Star Chamber Proc., Henry VIII, bundle 27, file 135.

4. TREASURER AND GOLDSMITH

1. *D.N.B.*

2. On this see my *Tudor Revolution in Government* (Cambridge, 1953), esp. pp. 169 ff.

3. The main papers in this case are these: the clerks' defence

prefaced by a transcript of Hayes' original charge (State Papers Henry VIII, vol. 121, fos. 209–28), together with two abstracts made of it (ibid. fos. 229–34); Hayes' reply (ibid. vol. 241, fos. 259–61); a letter from Sir Brian Tuke to Thomas Cromwell of 23 Dec. 1537 (ibid. vol. 127, fos. 117–18); and a file of Star Chamber papers of 1542–3 (Star Chamber Proc., Henry VIII, bundle 33, file 9). Detailed reference to these documents will not ordinarily be made: the story has to be extracted from them all in such a manner that full and repeated references would annoy and confuse rather than assist.

4. Star Chamber Proc., Henry VIII, bundle 33, file 9, doc. 4: depositions of 8 Feb. 1543.

5. 'Upon St. Anne's day or the morrow after.'

6. *L.P.* iv. 6748 (7, 11); *Addenda*, 439.

7. Cf. *L.P.* ix. 862, a report by Eustace Chapuys, imperial ambassador, of 21 Nov. 1535, that Tuke was living in the country and not coming to court. As usual, Chapuys tried to make out that Tuke's absence was caused by political motives – opposition to the break with Rome – but that was plainly nonsense.

8. These and the following details are derived from Tuke's letter with a little help from the defence (above, n. 3).

9. As appears from the part of the story which belongs to 1542–3.

10. For these documents see above, n. 3.

11. The angel was at this time a gold coin worth 10s., the crown a silver coin worth 5s.

12. My *Tudor Revolution in Government*, 180 f.

13. State Papers, Henry VIII, vol. 87, fo. 133. Some of Cromwell's own accounts are an almost inextricable mixture of private and public business.

14. 7, 13, 21, 31 March; 18, 28 April; 5, 9, 14 May. Nine payments for a total of £660. This sort of piecemeal working off is typical of an administration forced to rely on such cash as came in each day.

15. E.g., my *Tudor Revolution in Government*, 181 n. 1.

16. See above, n. 3.

17. *L.P.* xii. 1. 1235.

18. Above, n. 3.

19. His will was proved in 1547 (*Index of Wills proved in the Prerogative Court of Canterbury 1383–1558* [Index Library], 263).

20. *L.P.* xx. 11. 418(89); xxi. 1. 467.

21. *L.P. Add.* 1903.

22. *L.P.* xvi. 1028.

23. E.g., *L.P.* xix. 11. 166(72).

24. He was tenant of some houses in Aldwych in April 1553 (*Cal. Pat. Edward VI*, v. 112); in January 1559 these houses were described as 'once leased' to him (*Cal. Pat. Elizabeth*, i. 130). Of course, he may merely have terminated the lease, but at any rate I can find no further trace of him.

25. *L.P.* iv. 4518.

26. *L.P.* xv. 642, 862; xvi. 745 (fo. 52); xviii. 1. 436 (fos. 82, 89), 11. 231; xix. 1. 368 (fo. 52).

27. Cf. my *Tudor Revolution in Government*, 173 ff., 193 f., 233.

28. Ibid. 171 ff.

29. *L.P.* ix. 898.

30. *L.P.* xvi. 380 (fo. 152b).

31. *L.P.* xvi. 678 (8).

32. Above, p. 119.

33. Corp. of London, Record Office, Hustings Book 3 (1537–60), fo. 95. This calendar of all cases heard in this court makes no mention of Tuke's suit against Hayes.

5. QUONDAM OF RIEVAULX

1. W. Brown, 'Edward Kirkby, Abbot of Rievaulx', *Yorkshire Archaeological Journal*, xxi (1911), 44 ff.

2. E. Jeffries Davis, 'The Beginning of the Dissolution: Christ Church, Aldgate', *Trans. R. Hist. Soc.*, 1925, 127 ff.

3. D. Knowles and R. N. Hadcock, *Medieval Religious Houses* (1953), 114. The authors appear to have been misled by *Victoria County History, Yorkshire*, iii. 151 f. G. Baskerville, as one might expect, saw the matter in a light less favourable to the abbot, and for

once he was quite right: *English Monks and the Suppression of the Monasteries* (1937), 92, 164 f.

4. Cf. *The Register or Chronicle of Butley Priory, Suffolk* (ed. A. G. Dickens, 1951).

5. He appears to have held two vicarages in succession till his death in 1557: Baskerville, op. cit., 165 n.

6. State Papers, Henry VIII, vol. 76, fos. 14 and 27.

7. Ibid. fo. 130.

8. *L.P.* vi. 160.

9. Ibid. 562 (ii), 601.

10. State Papers, Henry VIII, vol. 238, fo. 155.

11. Ibid.

12. *L.P.* vii. 923 (xxi, xxxv).

13. Printed in *Memorials of the Abbey of St Mary of Fountains* (Surtees Soc., 1863), i. 260 f.

14. Baskerville, op. cit. 91.

15. *L.P.* v. 978 (6).

16. State Papers, Henry VIII, vol. 78, fo. 52.

17. Cooper, *Athenae Cantabrigienses*, i. 87 f.

18. Cf. Baskerville, op. cit. 126; but his extravances require some sceptical reassessment.

19. State Papers, Henry VIII; vol. 78, fos. 132–3.

20. Ibid. vol. 79, fo. 1.

21. *Memorials of Fountains*, i. 260–2.

22. The commission is recited in full at the head of the report made to the king by the abbot of Byland: Star Chamber Proc., Henry VIII, vol. 7, fo. 217. This has been printed, with some errors, in *Yorkshire Star Chamber Proceedings* (Yorks. Record Series, no. xli, 1909), 48 ff.

23. Brown (op. cit. 47) described this house as Benedictine, which would make the activities there of a Cistercian abbot rather odd; however, it was a Cistercian abbey all right.

24. The report of the abbot of Byland, Star Chamber Proc., Henry VIII, vol. 7, fo. 217.

25. State Papers, Henry VIII, vol. 238, fo. 155, report of Rutland's party.

26. Brown thought it significant that none of Kirkby's opponents 'ventured to assert that Kirkby had been properly deposed' (op. cit. 47). But the real issue lay in the new election.

27. State Papers, Henry VIII, vol. 238, fo. 155.

28. Merriman, *Cromwell's Letters*, i. 366 (no. 56).

29. State Papers, Henry VIII, vol. 80, fo. 198.

30. *Memorials of Fountains*, 263 f.

31. *L.P.* xiv. 1. 185.

32. State Papers, Henry VIII, vol. 100, fo. 116.

33. State Papers, Henry VIII, vol. 88, fo. 99.

34. *Memorials of Fountains*, i. 264.

35. 26 Henry VIII, c. 3.

36. State Papers, Henry VIII, vol. 100, fos. 115–16.

37. Ibid. vol. 125, fo. 118.

38. This is well worked out by Brown, op. cit. 50.

39. 26 Henry VIII, c. 1.

40. *L.P.* xiv. 1. 651 (43).

6. TITHE AND TROUBLE

1. M. Robbins, *Middlesex* (1953), 286.

2. Ibid. In 1545 Cranmer surrendered it to the crown in exchange for other lands (37 Henry VIII c. 16) and the long association came to an end.

3. R. Newcourt, *Repertorium Ecclesiasticum Parochiale Londinense* (1708), i. 638.

4. G. Hennessy, *Novum Repertorium Ecclesiasticum Parochiale Londinense* (1898), 209.

5. At least that is the sense I can make of the scanty data available: *Hist. MSS. Comm. Ninth Report*, 120b (petition of William Warham, rector of Hayes, for a perpetual vicarage in the parish church, endowed with a competent share of the tithe); Newcourt, *Repertorium*, i. 639.

6. The lease is known from the documents in the case to be discussed here in which Gold appears as farmer of the rectory; for his status as a lawyer cf. *L.P.* xi. 385 (32).

7. See below, p. 220.

8. J. A. Venn, *Alumni Cantabrigienses*; *L.P.* iii. 376, 2052, 2864; iv. 1140.

9. *L.P.* ii, App. 17.

10. Ibid. iii. 419.

11. *L.P.* iv. 2627.

12. It does not appear that any rector was appointed between Gold's collation in 1526 and his death in 1534 (Hennessy, *Novum Repertorium*, 209, 300).

13. *L.P.* iv. 2577, 2854, 3222, 3589; v. 198.

14. State Papers, Henry VIII, vol. 83, fo. 123.

15. The materials (hereafter referred to by the letters appended to them here) are: Archbishop Warham's bill in Star Chamber against certain villagers (Star Chamber Proc., Henry VIII, vol. 8, fo. 79: A); their answer and his replication (ibid. bundle 19, file 128, and bundle 18, file 254: A*); an interrogatory with depositions on Warham's behalf (ibid. bundle 17, file 387: B – a draft of part of this is in bundle 18, file 277); the depositions of Peter Lee, curate at Hayes, to this interrogatory and another (ibid. vol. 8, fos. 80–94: D); a summary of the evidence collected in the last two documents (ibid. vol. 9, fos. 29–32: C); Thomas Gold's articles exhibited in Star Chamber against certain villagers (ibid. vol. 16, fo. 104: E – an earlier incomplete version is in bundle 22, file 101); an answer to these from the defendants (ibid. vol. 16, fo. 105: E*); an appeal from the defendants in which they comment on some of the charges (State Papers, Henry VIII, vol. 83, fos. 123–4: F); interrogatories on Gold's behalf, with answers, concerning tithe (Star Chamber Proc., Henry VIII, vol. 16, fo. 106 [G] and fo. 109 [H]); further interrogatories concerning the legal struggle (ibid. bundle 19, file 385: I – drafts in bundle 22, file 92 and bundle 24, file 413); depositions to these last (ibid. bundle 24, file 157: J); the deposition of the archbishop's apparitor (ibid. vol. 16, fo. 112: K); further depositions on Gold's behalf (ibid. fos. 116–28: L); exceptions against Gold's witnesses (ibid. fo. 114: M); defendants' depositions (ibid. bundle 25, file 305: N); and a complaint against Gold (ibid. bundle 19, file 112: O).

16. Docs. F and M.

17. Docs. A* and E*.

18. Doc. E.

19. Doc. D.

20. Doc. L.

21. Doc. G.

22. Docs. H and L.

23. For the law governing tithe, settled but not changed at the Reformation, cf. W. Sheppard, *The Parson's Guide on the Law of Tithe* (1654), esp. pp. 17 and 19.

24. Ibid. 19.

25. 27 Henry VIII c. 20, 32 Henry VIII c. 7, 2 & 3 Edward VI c. 13.

26. Doc. N.

27. Doc. O.

28. Docs. E and I.

29. Docs. D and J.

30. Docs. L and N.

31. The story of Page emerges from docs. D, E, I, L and N.

32. Doc. D.

33. Doc. L.

34. According to Lee (D) and Faxton (L) who reported the words; others of Gold's witnesses only testified that the crowd used to go up to the vicarage.

35. Doc. E.

36. Doc. N.

37. For these events see docs. D, E, I and L.

38. Docs. A, B, C, D and K.

39. Doc. N.

40. Again the fullest deposition is Lee's (D) but much of the detail is confirmed by Gold's other witnesses (L).

41. Doc. N.

42. The material for the story of the injunction is the same as that for the citation, except that Dodworth (K) only testified to the latter.

43. Burbage was probably a landowner in Hayes and the only rival to Gold as a substantial and independent man. Page, it will be remembered, had thought both their houses worth investigation (above, p. 189), and Burbage at some time had a quarrel with Canterbury over some copyhold lands which the archbishop claimed ought to be held of the manor of Hayes (Star Chamber Proc., Henry VIII, vol. 8, fo. 78).

44. Doc. N.

45. Doc. F.

46. For the story of the precept see docs. A, B, C, D and N.

47. For the dismissal of Lee see the same documents as for the precept.

48. Doc. A.

49. Doc. A*. The defendants also maintained that the matter at issue should be tried at common law or in the spiritual courts, but that reservation was common form in Star Chamber answers and has no special significance.

50. Docs. E and E*.

51. Cf., e.g., the analysis in A. Ogle, *The Tragedy of the Lollards' Tower* (1949), 260 ff. His attack on More's activities certainly fits the facts and the temper of the time better than does, e.g., R. W. Chambers' rather tortuous defence in *Sir Thomas More* (1948 repr.), 274 ff.

52. Doc. F. The paper can have got to its present place among the state papers only in one of two ways: either Henry Gold had a copy which was confiscated when he was later arrested, or it was part of Cromwell's archives. The latter supposition is much the more likely and would help to identify the addressee, but proof is impossible.

53. Some suggestion of his stand in such matters may be seen in the fact that as early as 1528 a friend of his wrote specifically to condemn Tyndale's translation of the New Testament (*L.P.* iv. 3960).

54. For a good account of the whole episode see K. Pickthorn, *Early Tudor Government* (1934), ii. 217 ff.

55. 25 Henry VIII c. 12.

56. *L.P.* vii. 522.

57. State Papers, Henry VIII, vol. 82, fo. 150.

58. *L.P.* v. 1378.

59. State Papers, Henry VIII, vol. 92, fos. 192–3.

60. In Cranmer's letter the name was John Creake, but the same man was probably meant.

61. *L.P.* xi. 385 (32).

INDEX